Fashion Model Photography
Professional Images and Techniques

Billy Pegram

AMHERST MEDIA, INC. ■ BUFFALO, NY

Published by:
Amherst Media, Inc.
P.O. Box 586
Buffalo, N.Y. 14226
Fax: 716-874-4508

Publisher: Craig Alesse
Senior Editor/Project Manager: Richard Lynch
Associate Editor: Michelle Perkins

ISBN: 0-936262-78-8
Library of Congress Card Catalog Number: 98-72987

Printed in the United States of America.
10 9 8 7 6 5 4 3 2 1

Notice of Disclaimer: The information contained in this book is based on the author's experience and opinions. The author and publisher will not be held liable for the use or misuse of the information in this book.

The publisher wishes to thank Frank McDaniel for his role in the inception of this book.

Dedication

I dedicate this book to all the people who were willing to give freely of their time, knowledge and equipment to help me learn and pursue this career. I would like to encourage established photographers and agents to help beginning photographers learn our craft.

Special thanks to Loa Anderson, Dennis Bergum, David Brooks, and Ron Miller.

Table of Contents

Interview with Billy Pegram

How did you get started in photography?
When I was in seventh grade, I moved to a new junior high. One of the teachers there was also my scout master. He needed a student photographer that he could trust with keys to the school, so he approached my parents and said, "Can I turn your son into a photographer?"

By high school I was doing a lot of photography, mostly sports, but I never really thought of photography as a career. I went to college and studied medicine, then worked in medical research.

Eventually I heard about a photography contest and I entered. I won first, second, third, fifth, sixth and seventh places, and about $4000. That's when I started thinking about whether I would rather spend my life with pretty girls or sick people!

How did you become interested in fashion photography?
As I said, I started out doing a lot of sports photography, and I really loved doing that. The problem was, doing journalistic sports photography, you have a lot of trouble getting paid. With fashion photography you are paid up front for the work you do. I also find it is a more creative form of photography.

So, about ten years ago, having made this decision, I approached a friend of mine who was teaching at a modeling school and offered to do a test shoot. As luck would have it, the owner had just had a fight with her regular photographer and they took me up on my offer. This gave me access to a full studio and darkroom!

In the course of your career you've moved around quite a bit. What are some of the places you've worked?
After working at the modeling school, I moved on to Los Angeles to work. That's where I got my first major contract with Swatch Watch USA.

From there I moved to Seattle because a friend of mine owned a record label there and asked me to come up and shoot his bands. I really wanted to go commercial and work more with models, but Seattle offers hard weather for shooting and the fashion industry there is not terribly strong.

That was when I heard about Phoenix. All of the major modeling agencies were setting up there, and it was getting to be an important area for model shooting. Unfortunately, it never quite reached the point that was anticipated, since most people decided to fly in for shoots, rather than set up a permanent operation there. I did get an important contract there, though, with Fila athletic shoes.

At the moment I'm actually in the process of another move to Monterey, California, where I'm setting up a new studio.

What kinds of work besides fashion photography have you (or do you) done?

I've done just about every kind of work that involves shooting people. I do a lot of PR work and quite a bit of fine art photography. I also find that I'm doing more sports photography than ever, although no longer from a journalistic angle. Now I take a lot of photographs for athletes to use in their promotional materials. I also do product shots occasionally, usually in conjunction with shooting a model. It's easier for companies to have me do both the model and the product shot than to hire two photographers. A big part of my work now is scouting models and getting them ready to work professionally.

What kind of equipment do you prefer?

I sometimes use a medium format camera for commercial assignments, but I prefer a 35mm format for shooting people because it's simply a lot faster to use than a medium format. I generally use either a Nikon F3 or FE2 camera. The FE2 is what I prefer to use outdoors, since the flash synchs at 1/250 second.

I also use Nikon lenses. In the studio I usually go for the 85mm or 105mm. For head shots I prefer a 135-200mm. On location I use a 300mm lens as much as possible.

I rarely use anything but Kodak Elite 100 film for color work. I used to use professional film all the time, but since I started working in high temperatures I have started using over the counter products. Professional film shifts quickly in extreme temperatures. When shooting on location, this can be a big hassle (especially when the black camera itself can get very hot). However, if I'm shooting indoors on an assignment where color matching is important, I do use professional film.

For black and white work, I use Kodak Plus X, or TMAX 100. I also like Agfa 100, but find it's hard to get when working on location.

I usually use a Bogen tripod. When I'm shooting people I want to be able to watch their expression and not have to constantly look to see that the horizon is level.

What are your plans for the future?

The new studio in Monterey will allow me to pursue additional opportunities in the field of multimedia by producing videos in select applications of health and wellness. I also plan to pursue opportunites in publication of photography books and to teach and lecture whenever possible.

■ Assignment

This photograph was taken as part of an ad campaign for a hairdresser. He wanted a very urban looking image. Like many of my clients, he let me basically work as the art director, as well as the photographer.

■ Location

The image was shot in the shaded alleyway next to the hair salon.

■ Posing

The posing of the model in this image was designed to minimize the appearance of her hips. Pointing her toe helps to lengthen and slim her leg, while her raised knee makes the viewer's eye move across the image vertically (rather than horizontally). The ripped jeans add to this effect.

■ Photography

A Nikon F3 camera was used with a 200mm lens. The exposure was 1/30 second at f-8. I used Kodak Elite 100 film, rated at 80. A little overexposure helps to create the look of very clear, flawless skin.

■ Lighting

This was a lovely Seattle day, and the sun had just dropped below the horizon. The street in which we were shooting was shadowed by a building. Shot only with this natural light, the only necessary adjustment for lighting purposes was to pose the model with her face tilted up to avoid creating eye socket shadows.

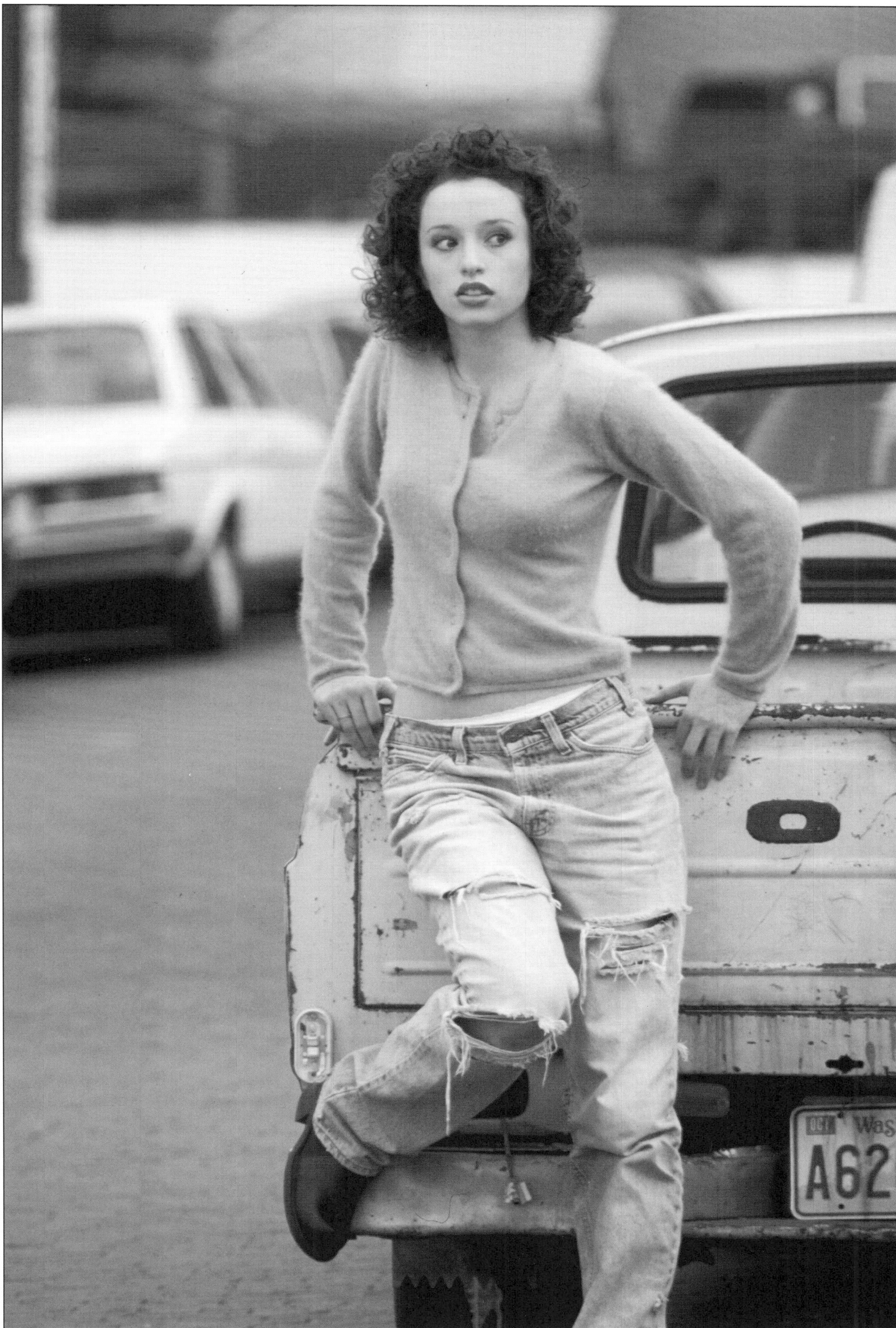

■ Posing

As often happens on shoots, the clothes didn't fit the model. In this case, the pants were too baggy, and too short. The pose selected helps to minimize the appearance of the poor fit of the clothing, and to show off the model's long legs.

Clothes not fitting is something that occurs frequently and has to be worked around. When working with designer samples that are made overseas, the clothes generally arrive with a cut on them. This is done so that the garments can be shipped as samples (saving the cost of import tax). Because of this fact, it is frequently necessary to add a makeshift seam to the back of a shirt, or take a few tucks to make a garment fit. Still, you won't want to shoot areas which have been mended in this way, so you have to be flexible with posing.

The model's raised hand also adds a sense of energy and movement to the image.

■ Lighting

The lighting set-up for this photograph consists of two Norman umbrellas which were placed at 45° angles from the subject who was posed on white, seamless paper.

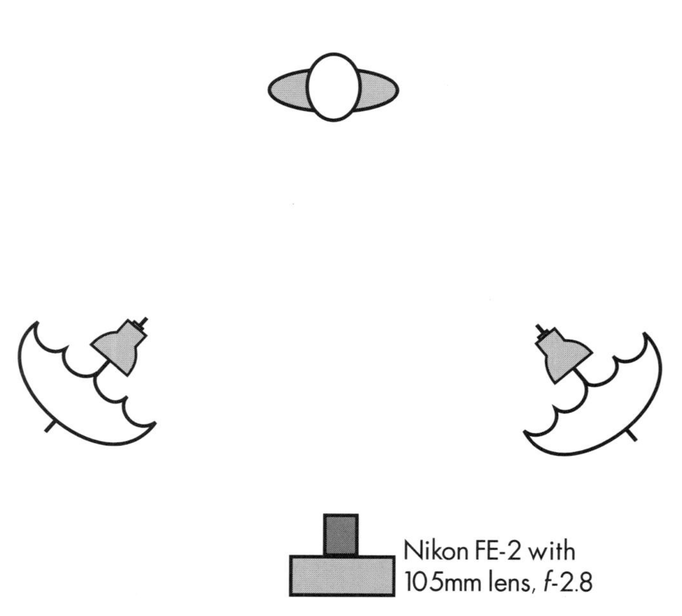

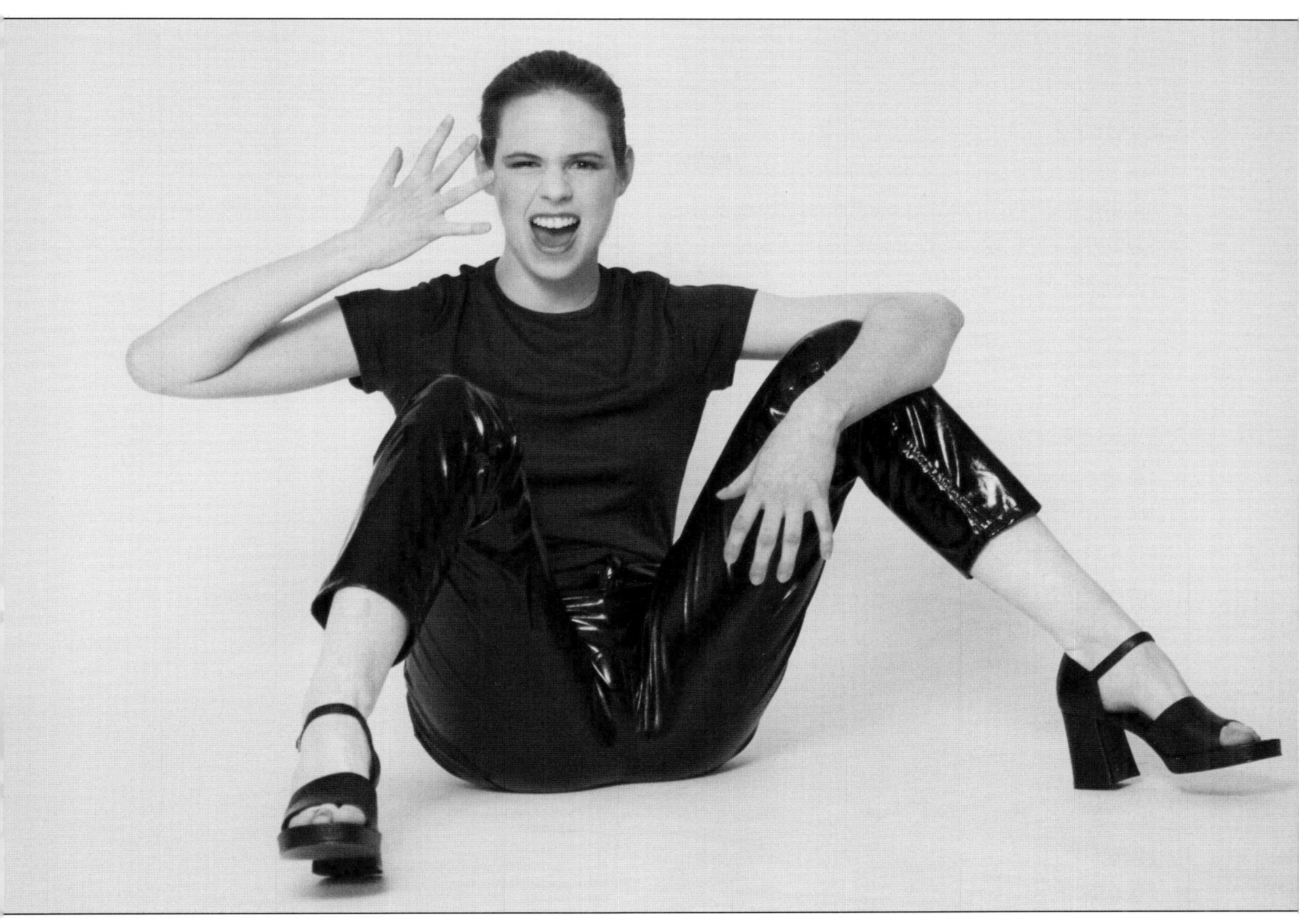

■ Posing

The model was posed with her knees tucked up while sitting in a beanbag chair in her living room. The image was taken to be used by the model in her portfolio.

■ Photography

The photograph was shot with a Nikon FE2 camera using a 105mm lens and Ektachrome tungsten 160 speed film which I rated at 125. The exposure was 1/60 second at f-8. I also used an 80A filter which, when used with tungsten film, creates a blue cast. The shot was metered at 11 but shot at 8 to slightly overexpose it. The camera was positioned above the model to shoot the image.

■ Lighting

The only light source was an umbrella placed over the model.

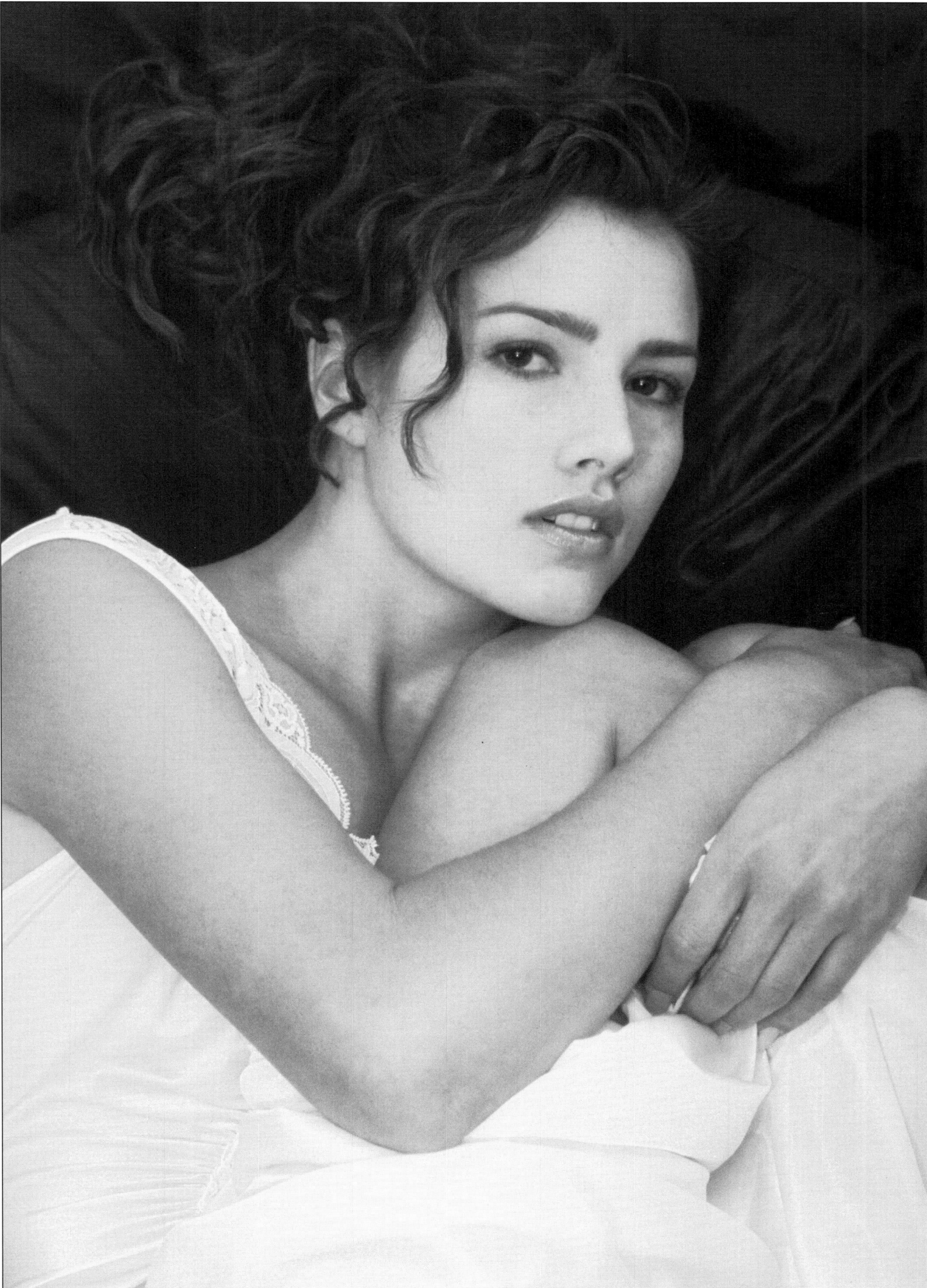

■ Assignment

This image was taken as part of a series of photographs for a female body builder. She was entering a competition and had to provide photographs of various parts of her physique.

■ Background

The background is a 4' x 4' sheet of colored plastic (such as you might see on floats in parades).

■ Photography

For this image, I used a Nikon FE-2 camera with a 200 mm lens at f-4. The film used was Elite 100, rated at 80.

■ Lighting

A bare Norman bulb was placed to the left of the model, shining on the background. It was goboed so as to prevent the light from hitting the camera. A soft box was used to the right of the model and creates the light you see on that hip.

■ Posing

The model was rubbed down with baby oil and spritzed with water to create the beaded sheen on her skin.

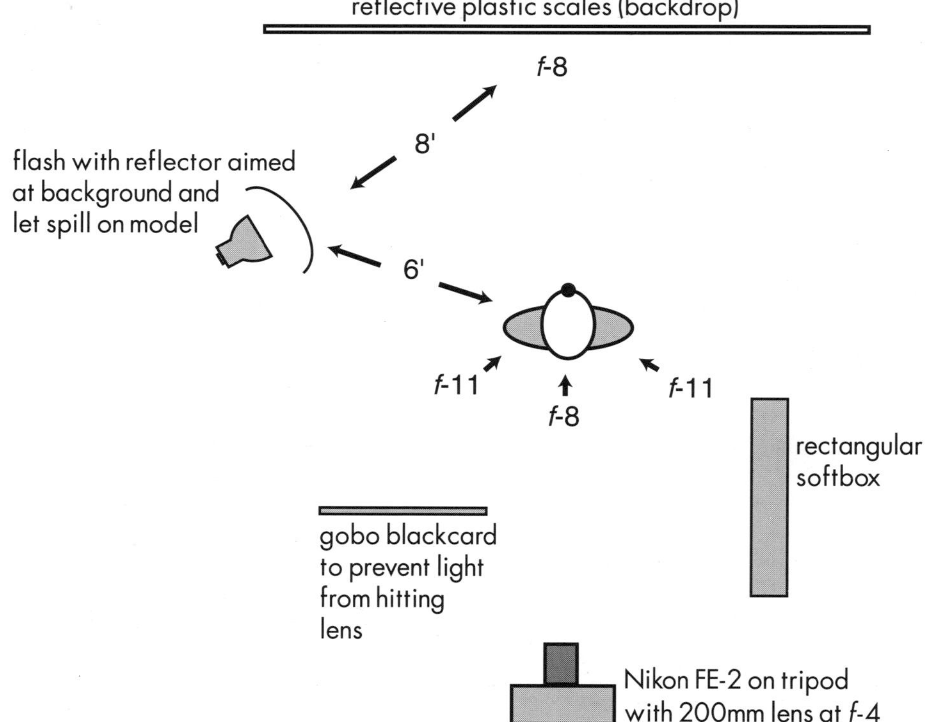

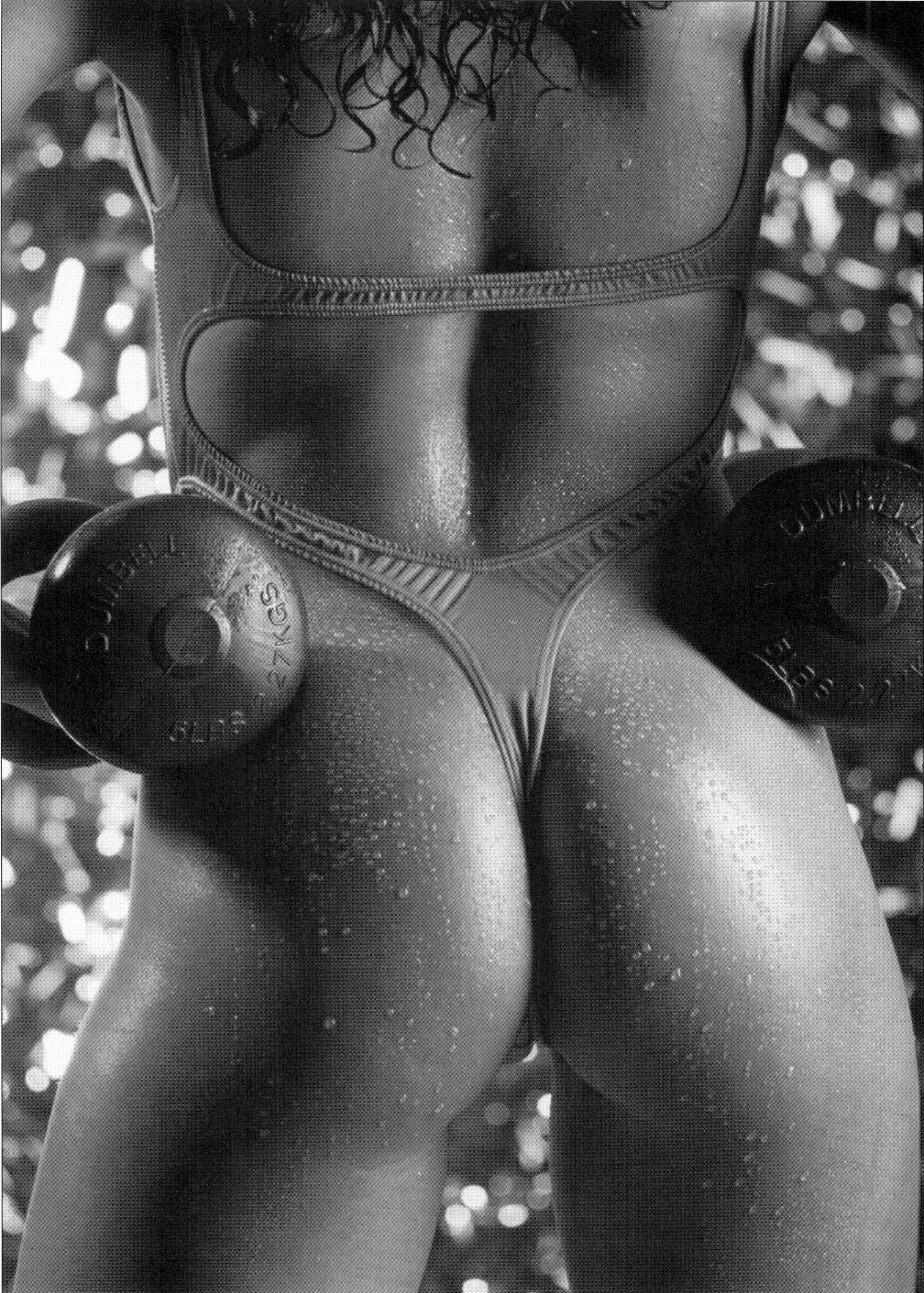

DUMBELL 5LBS 2.27KGS
DUMBELL 5LBS 2.27K

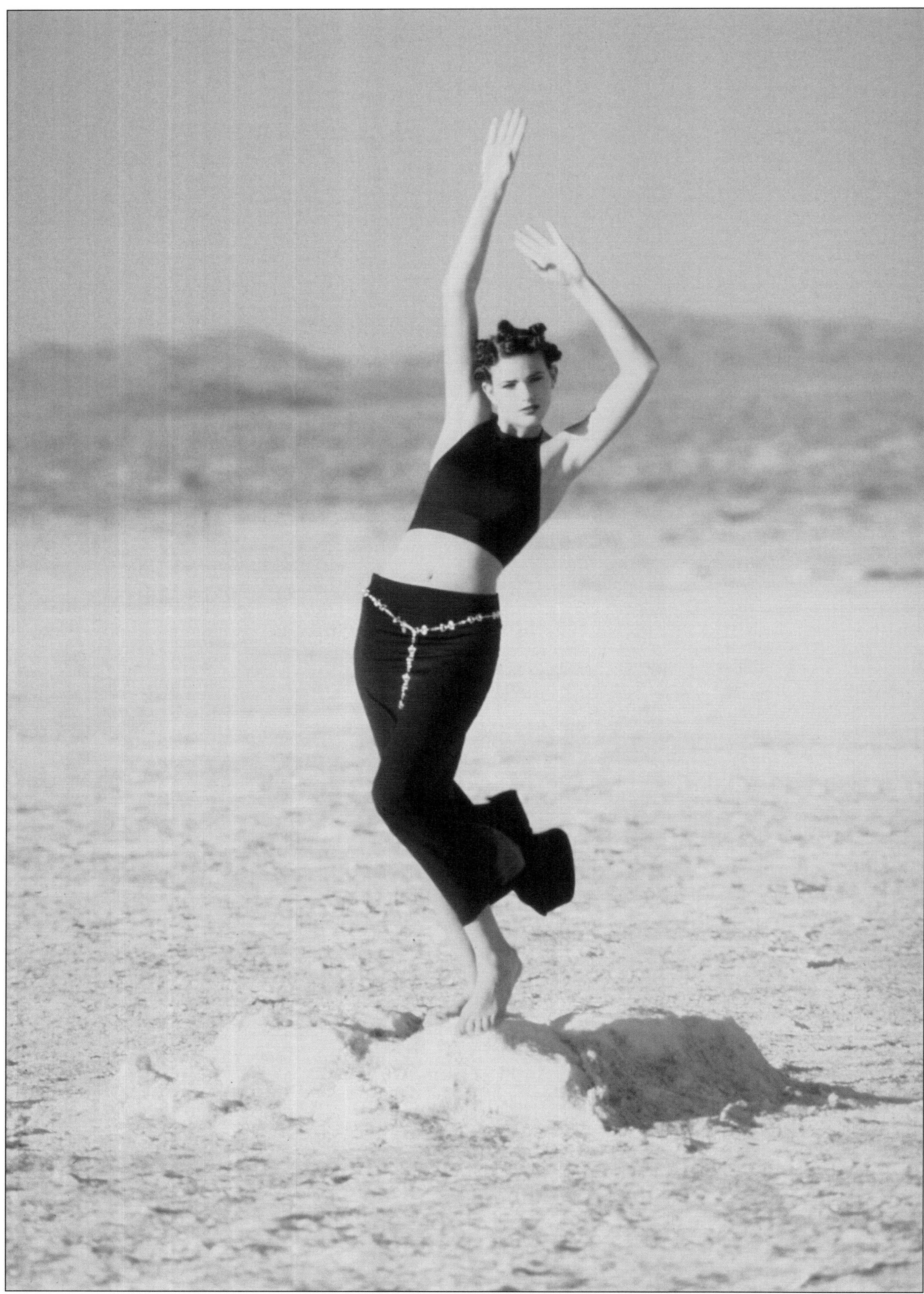

■ Assignment

I rarely use models from agencies, since I prefer to find my own models and then train them. This means I do a lot of shoots for models' portfolios. This is one such image. This model was getting ready to go to Europe, and I wanted to give her some versatile images that would really stand out — images you just couldn't get in Milan. Therefore, I shot this photo in the salt flats of Utah. The final image was also cross processed, a technique that will be described in detail on page 32.

■ Posing

The model is standing on a mound of salt. Because the sun was bright, she posed with her eyes closed until I was ready to snap the photo, then I had her open her eyes for the exposure.

■ Photography

This image was shot using a Nikon FE2 camera with a 300mm lens (the lens I use on location wherever possible). The Nikon FE2 is a good camera for shooting outdoors since the flash synchs at 1/250 of a second.

■ Assignment

Fashion photography has elements of commercial photography, but also of art photography. As a fashion photographer, you have to ask yourself, "What are we trying to sell?" as well as "What are we trying to emphasize?" When working on portfolio shots for a model, this means identifying that model's saleable assets and emphasizing them.

■ Posing

Since it was raining outside, we moved the shoot indoors and posed the model on white seamless paper. This pose shows off one of this model's strongest assets — her legs.

■ Photography

To get the right perspective, I shot the model from above while standing on a ladder. I used a 35mm lens.

■ Working with Models

An important thing to keep in mind when photographing models (especially inexperienced ones) is to make the shoot comfortable for them, since being in front of the camera can be intimidating. I love making models feel the confidence they need to be at their best on camera. I do this by focusing on their strengths and getting them pumped up about the shoot. I also use stories to make it clear to them that being in front of a camera in the studio isn't like being in front of mom's camera at a picnic. One of my favorite stories is about a Sports Illustrated swimsuit photographer who shot 40,000 pictures on location to get 60 for print — and that was with a full make-up and hair crew, photographic assistants and professional models! Not every photo has to be perfect! In a portfolio or glamour shoot, it also helps to remind your models that no one will see the photo before them, so if they hate a particular image, they can choose not to use it. Of course, this is not true for professional shoots, where models normally won't see the photographs until they are published.

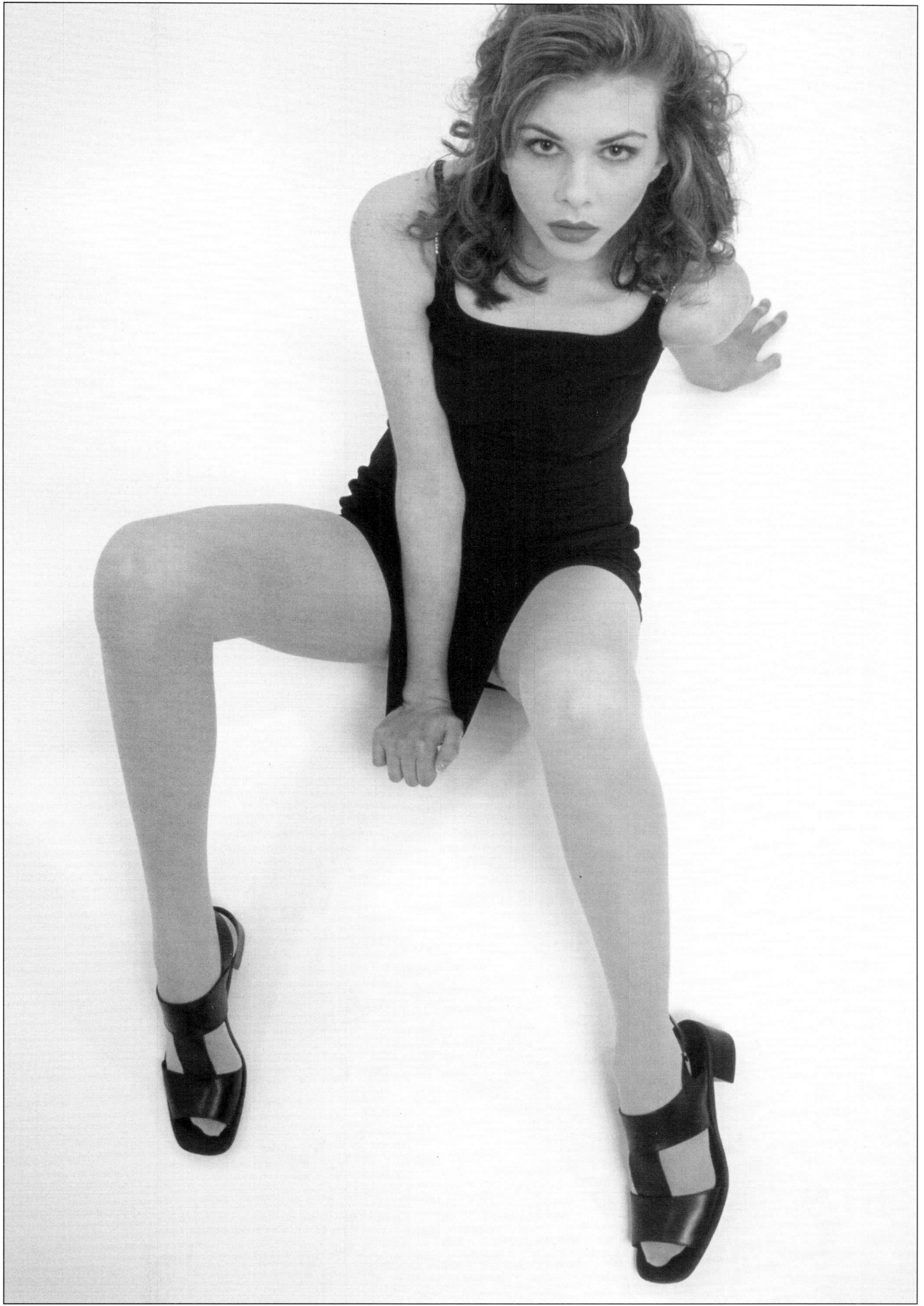

■ Assignment

I had a project coming up for a gun poster, so I decided to go out and scout some possible locations for the shoot. Since this was just a test shoot, we went out with no make-up, no special hair treatments and no lighting equipment. Although the site tested out well, on the day of the actual shoot, it was simply too hot to use it. We ended up shooting near a lake instead.

■ Lighting

The lighting is all available ligh. All I had to do was pose the models facing the sun.

■ Photography

The camera used was a Nikon FE2, with a 135 mm lens. I used Elite 100 film, and a 1/125 second exposure at f-11.

■ 35mm Cameras

For most of my work with models, I prefer the fast advance of a 35mm camera. I find that medium format is just too slow for shooting people, especially when you're asking them to do things like hold their eyes open in bright sunlight! I also always use a tripod. This helps me devote my attention to the models and increases the sharpness of the image.

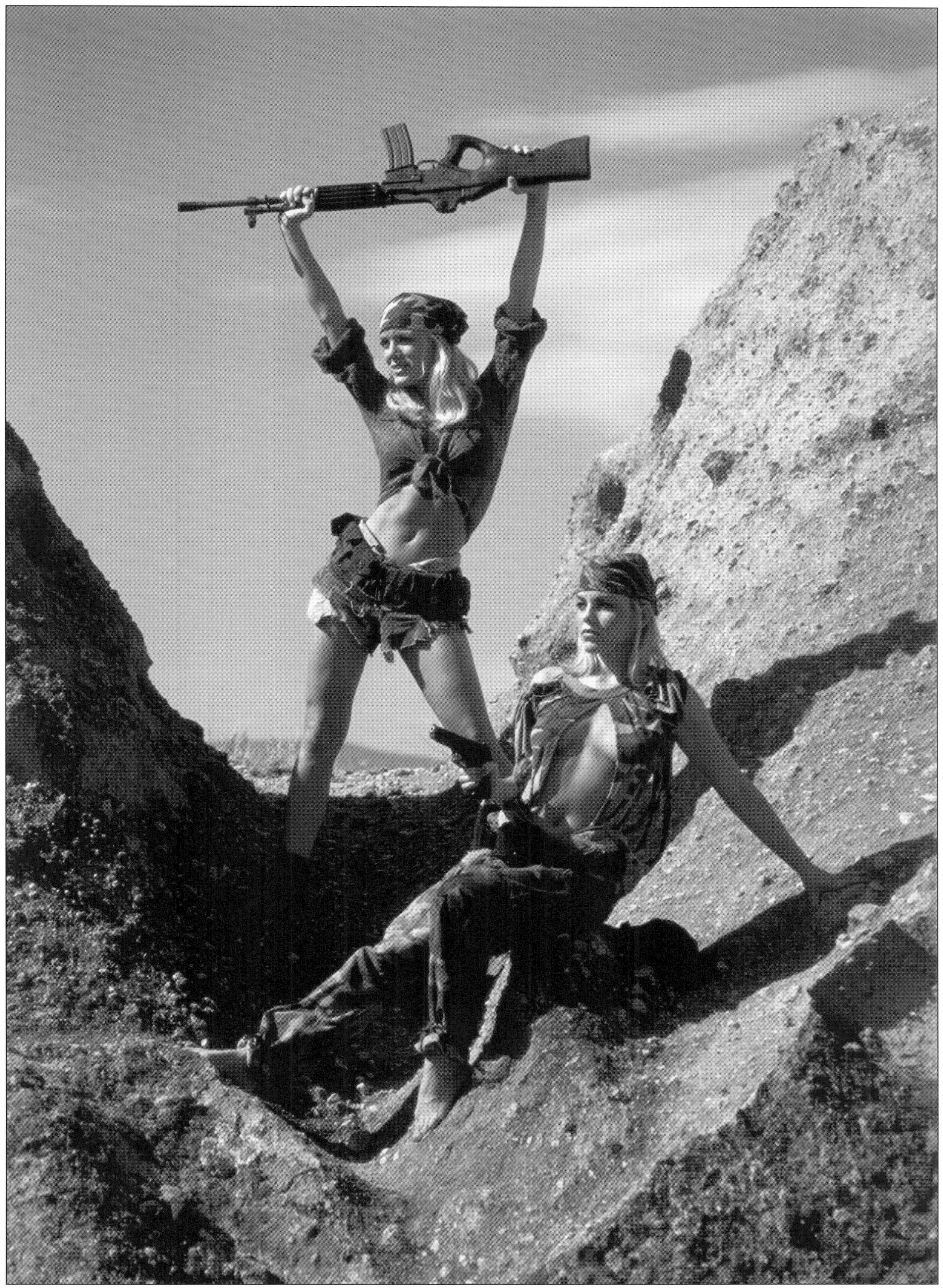

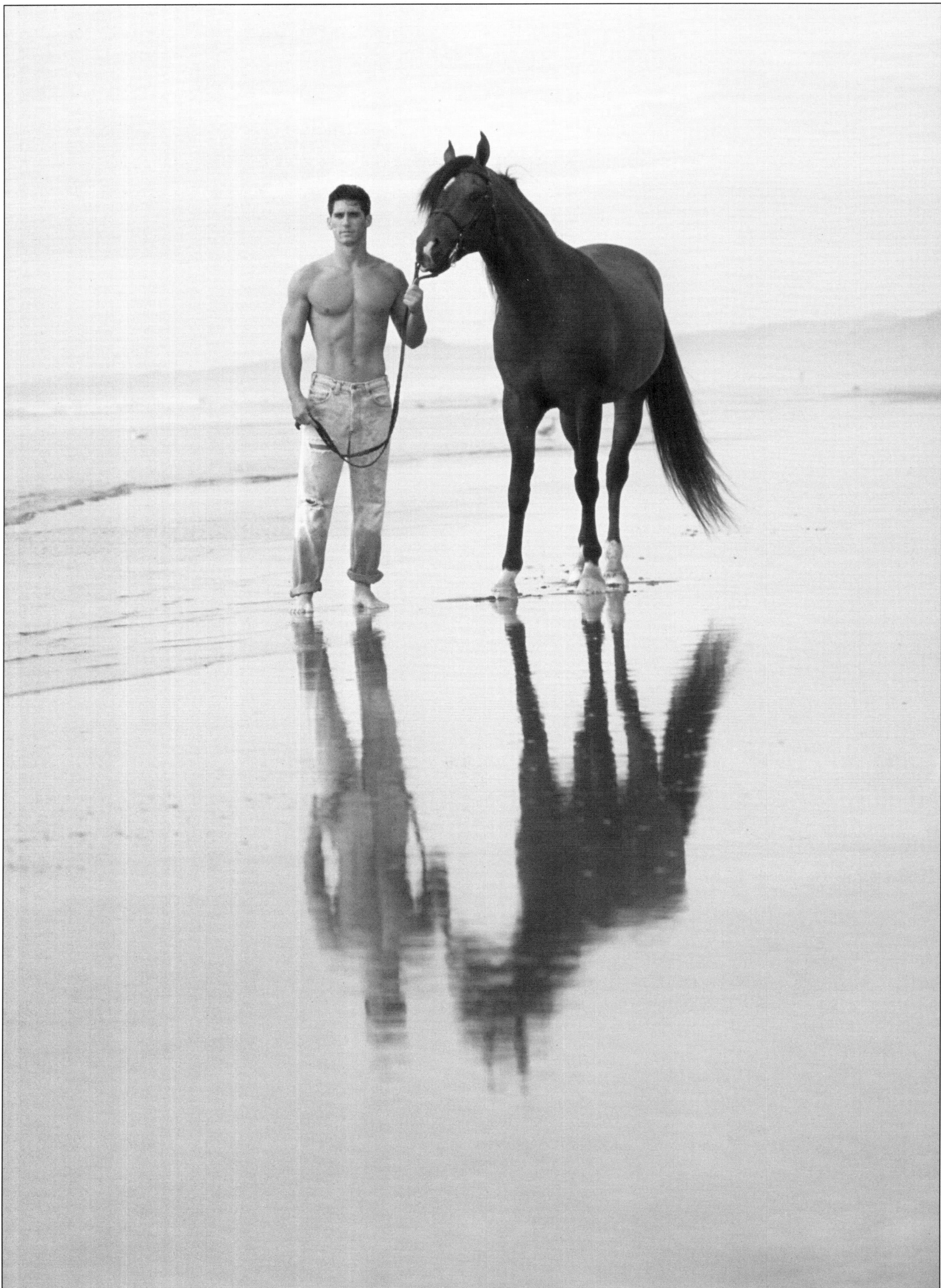

■ Assignment

This shoot was to take pictures for this model's portfolio. We went out and spent the whole day shooting.

■ Shooting Male Models

I shoot male models frequently, and there are several guidelines I follow. Unlike female models, male model's portfolios do not need to show as wide a range of looks or emotions. Men should be photographed looking very casual. Photos should also work off the shape of the model's jaw. A little powder will suffice for make-up. The idea is to convey a message of power, almost treating the model like a solid, strong piece of sculpture. If the image is shirtless, as here, side lighting is desirable to create harder lines and show off the chest physique.

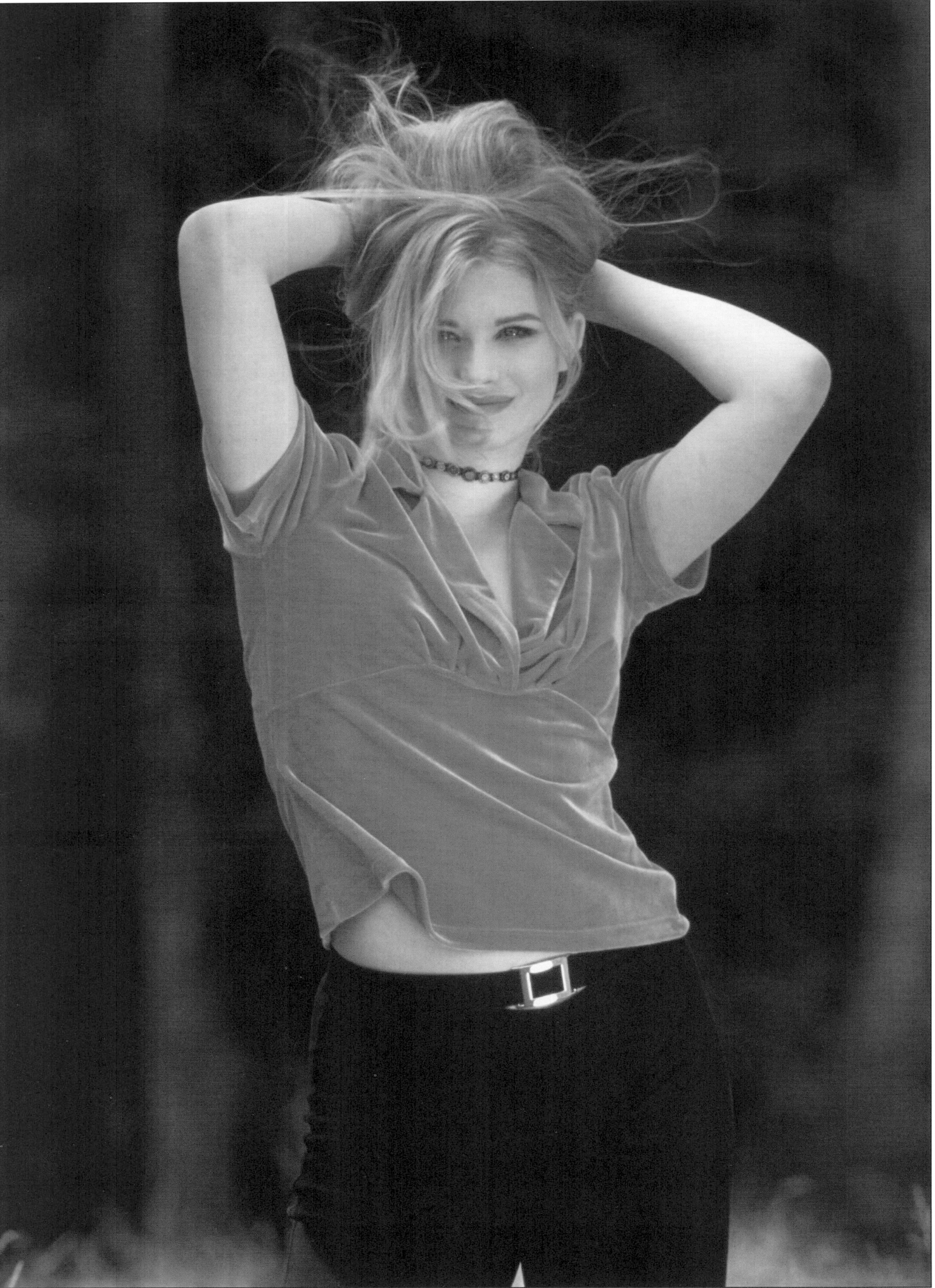

■ Assignment

This was this model's first shoot, and she was only 12 years old. A few months later, she had a contract in Europe!

■ Photography

I used a Nikon FE2 camera with Elite 100 film, rated at 80. The exposure was 1/60 second at f-5.6 1/2. I also used a 300mm lens which allows the background to drop out of the image.

■ Lighting

The sunlight was streaming over her shoulders and a silver reflector was placed to the right, as close as possible to the frame, to add light to both sides of her body.

■ Working with New Models

One of the benefits of working with new models (who pay comparatively little for a session), is that I get to do a little experimentation with new looks, locations, poses, lighting, etc.. This means that when I am working for a corporate client, I don't have to spend as much time experimenting with the set-up then!

■ Assignment

This image was shot for the model's portfolio.

■ Lighting

The model was posed against a white wall. An umbrella under a Norman head was placed up next to the wall to create the shadow.

■ Posing

This pose was designed to show off the model's flat stomach. She is leaning quite far back and has one leg extended, a position which tightens and flattens the stomach. We also wet her hair to give it a little more dimension, and wet her shirt to make it cling slightly to the curves of her body and show off her breasts and stomach.

■ Hands

A basic rule for hands is to make sure they are never both at the same level. You should also be careful to keep the model's hands away from any problem area of her body. Placing hands there only draws extra attention to the area!

■ Make-up

Hair and make-up work is often done by the girls themselves, or by professional artists. I also do it occasionally. I have taken classes on the subject so that I can feel comfortable with doing the make-up at the last minute if I have to, but also so that I can better communicate with the make-up artists who are preparing the girls for the shoot.

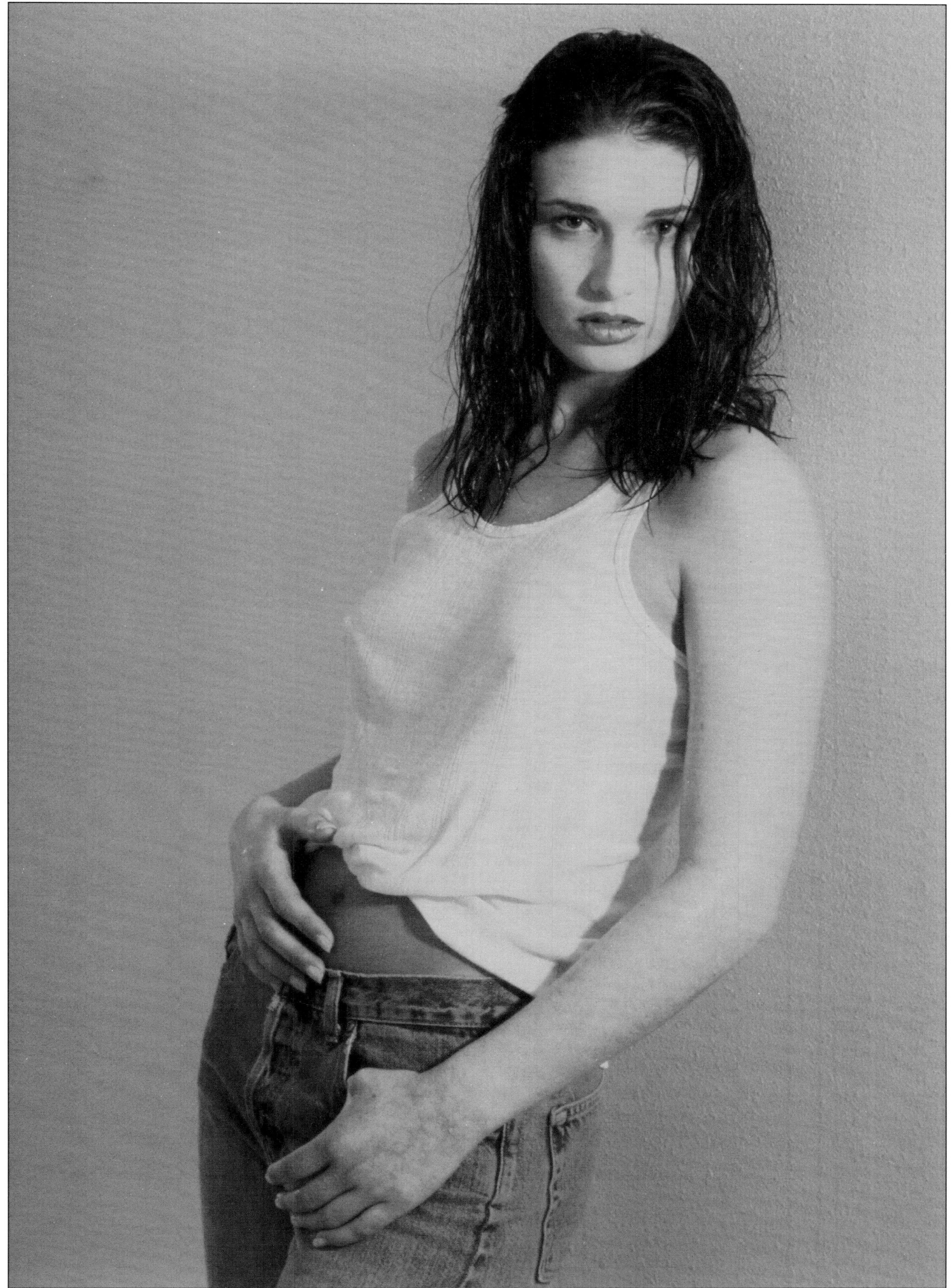

■ Assignment

This photograph was shot for the model's portfolio. It was her first photo session.

■ Pose

This pose was used to highlight the model's face, and especially her lips. Her eyes are closed so that they do not distract the viewer's attention from her lips and face. Her arms also frame her face, and further focus the viewer's eyes.

■ Lighting

The image was shot against white seamless paper. When shooting against white paper, it's important to remember that, while a model's skin reflects only about 36% of the light that hits it, the white paper reflects about 96%. This means that the light on the background should be about 1 to 2 stops less than the light on the model.

■ Portfolios

When shooting images for a model's portfolio, I have them bring a lot of clothes to the studio (better too many than too few!). The clothes you finally decide on should be ones that are not too trendy. Clothes like these will look dated quickly and require more photographs be taken. Once a model is well established she can add more trendy items to her portfolio. For the amateur model, try to accomplish a few basic shots: a basic head shot, a glamour head shot, a basic full body shot, etc.. Try to show the model's simple beauty with a clean and fresh look.

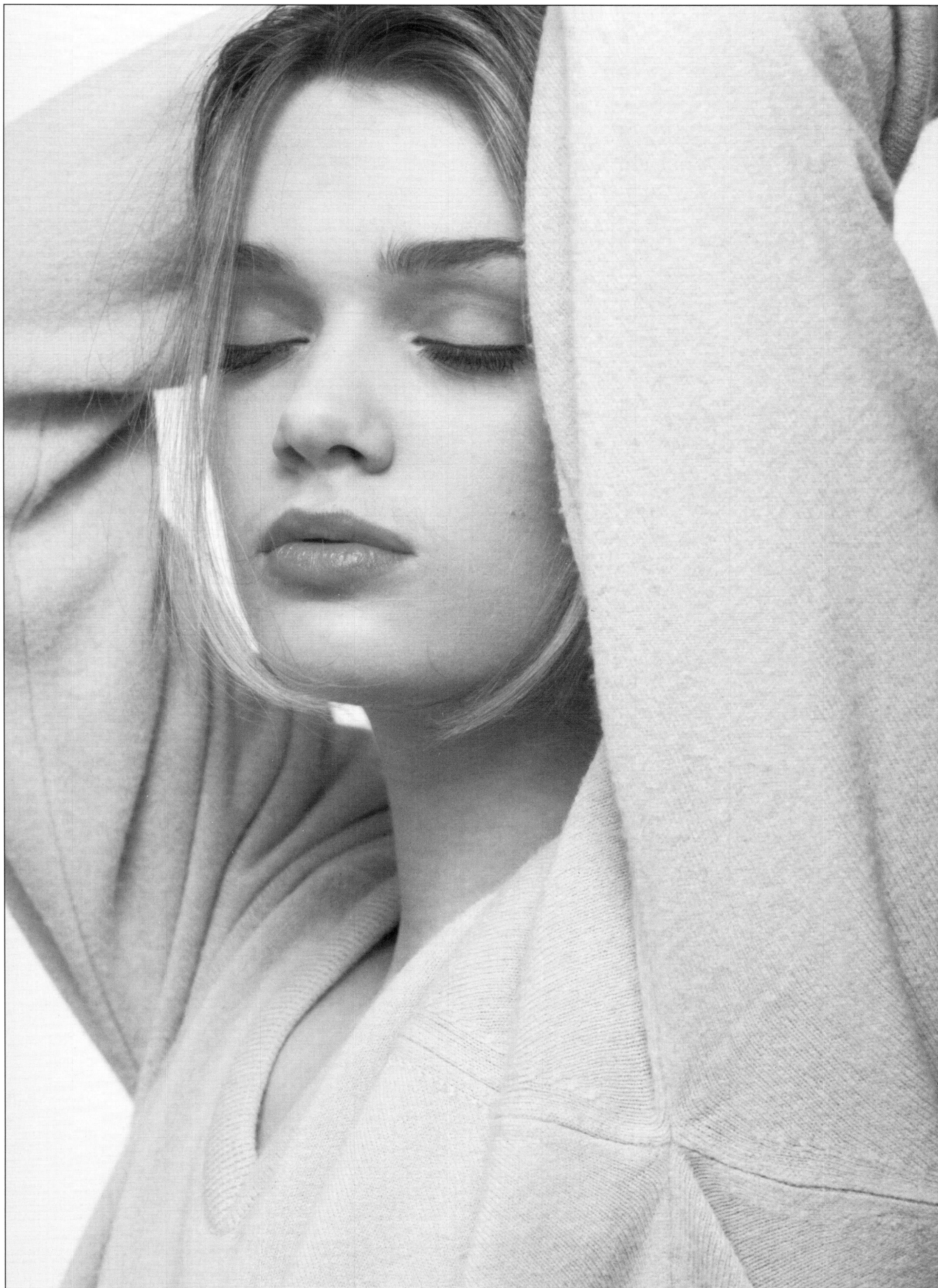

■ Assignment

This image was taken for the model's portfolio.

■ Pose

This model is very tall, so the pose and the low camera angle show off that great height.

■ Photography

Elite 100 film was rated at 80 for slight overexposure. A Nikon FM camera was used with a 300mm lens. Shooting at f-5.6 provides a nice degree of separation from the background, and keeps the model the focal point of the image (even with this potentially distracting background).

■ Lighting

We were shooting late in the day as the sun was going down and creating a nice golden light. I placed a gold disc reflector to the right of the model to help balance that light.

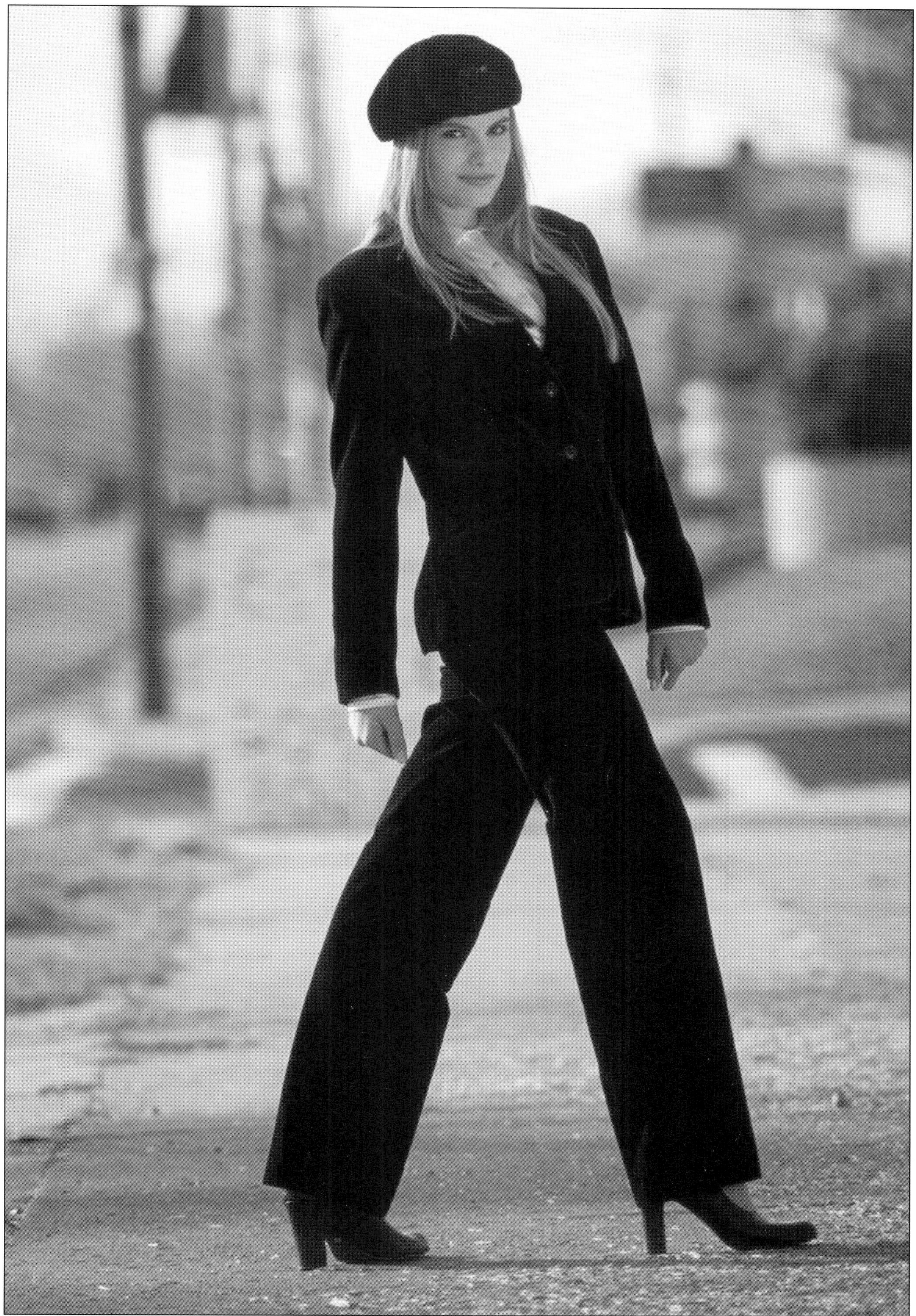

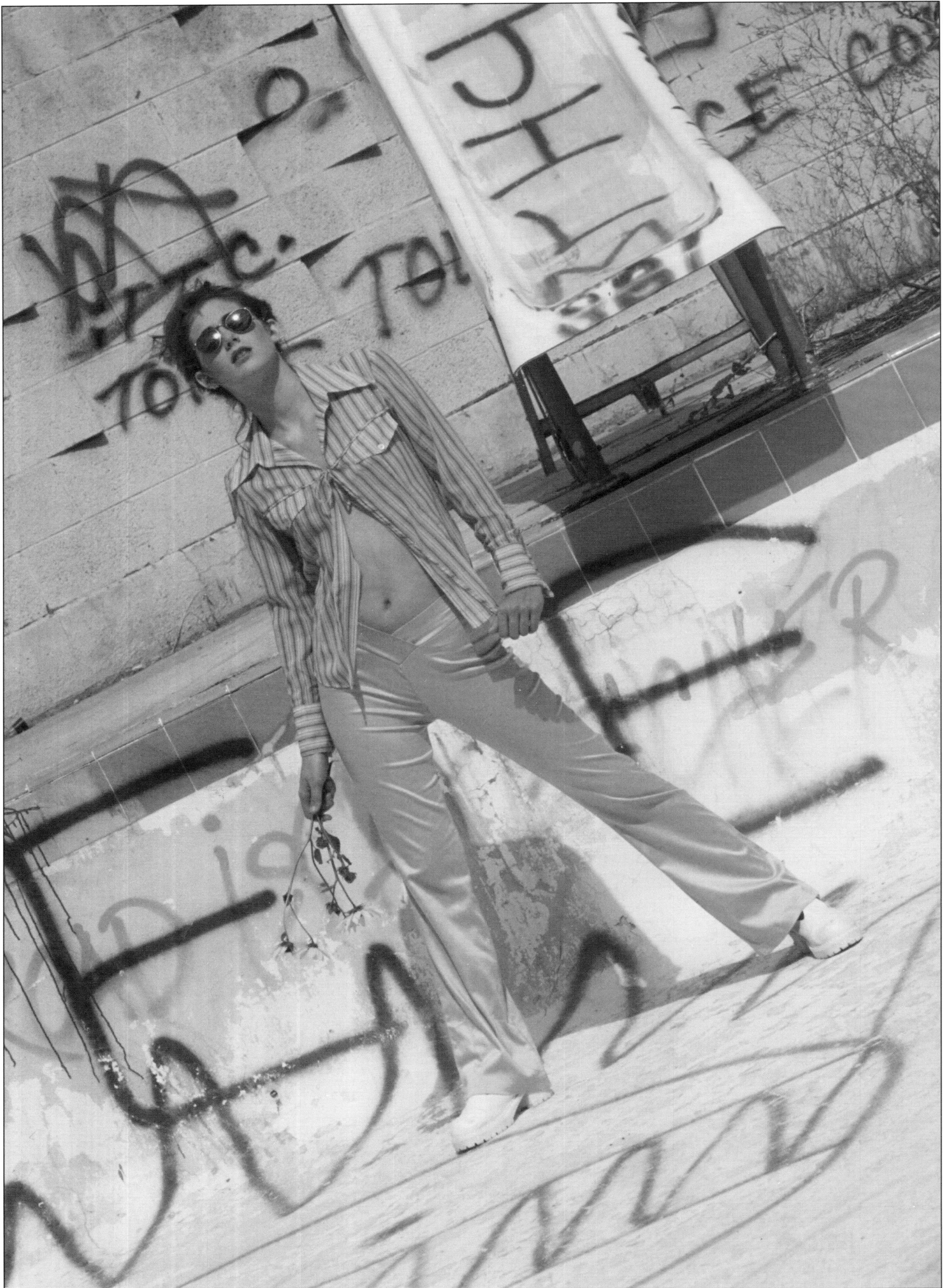

■ Assignment

This image was shot for the model's portfolio.

■ Composition

The model's pose works well with the slide. The viewer's eye moves from the slide to her kicked-out hip, back to the slide, back to the hip, and so on. The reflection on her sunglasses adds a nice area of interest to the image, and the flowers help to separate the model's hand from her leg.

■ Location

We had been shooting in a nearby field when I decided that the color of her outfit (a bright green) wasn't working well with the field. Therefore we moved to this nearby grafitti-covered swimming pool (which was about to be demolished).

■ Photography

I used a Nikon FM camera with a 200 mm lens. I shot the image at f-11 in order to make the writing show up clearly. The camera was also tilted slightly to create an interesting visual effect that compliments the composition.

■ Assignment

This photograph was taken for the model's portfolio.

■ Photography

The image was shot using Kodak VPS 160 rated at 80. The camera was tilted slightly to create a better flow of the eye across the page.

■ Lighting

One umbrella on a Norman flash was used. I positioned the umbrella as low as I could and still be able to shoot under the edge.

■ Cross Processing

Cross processing involves processing film in the wrong chemistry (for instance, processing print film as slide film). Every film responds completely differently. VPS print film processed as slide film creates a nice salmon cast that works well for skin; doing the same to Fuji 100 results in a green cast that isn't attractive for headshots (but is great for fantasy effects). After about 20 rolls of experiments, I have a reliable system for producing a nice color cast. I shoot VPS 160 rated at 80, then push it two stops in processing. It's important to tell your lab exactly what kind of film you have and how you want it E-6 processed. Since processing the film this way may mess up the lab's chemistry, they want to process it as the last roll of the day. An important note: with the new E-6 machines, images don't stay in the fixer long enough for this process to work. Images cross processed like this will need to be fixed twice or they will be dark and streaky. Kodak has sent out a memo on this, but it won't hurt to remind the lab!

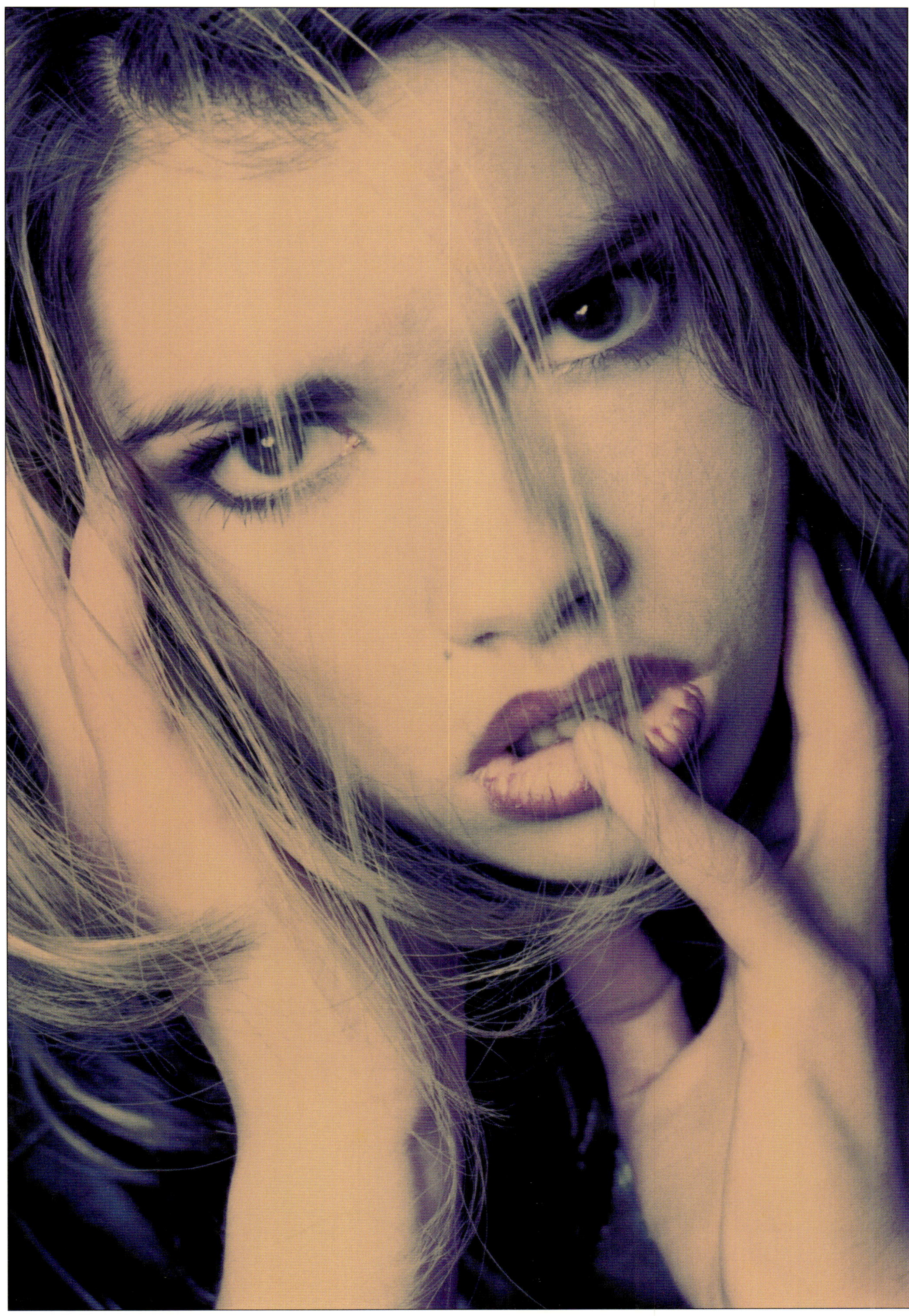

■ Assignment

This image was for the model's portfolio.

■ Composition

This was, by necessity, a tight shot since we only had a fur hat and stole to work with (rather than a whole fur coat.

■ On the Set

As you can see from the photo below, everyone gets involved with the shoot, including the model's mom who is holding the reflector. I do encourage models to bring a friend or parent to the studio, but generally I have them sit outside the room. Having an audience tends to make the models feel a little self-conscious, and less responsive to what I ask them to do. If the model's escort is in the room, I try to get him or her involved in the shoot — holding a reflector or light meter, for instance. This makes them more part of the crew and somehow less distracting to the model.

■ Lighting

An umbrella was positioned over the camera and a gold disc reflector was positioned under the model's chin. A white reflector was used to the model's right. A stream of water is held in the background. Although it is barely visible, it adds a nice sense of depth.

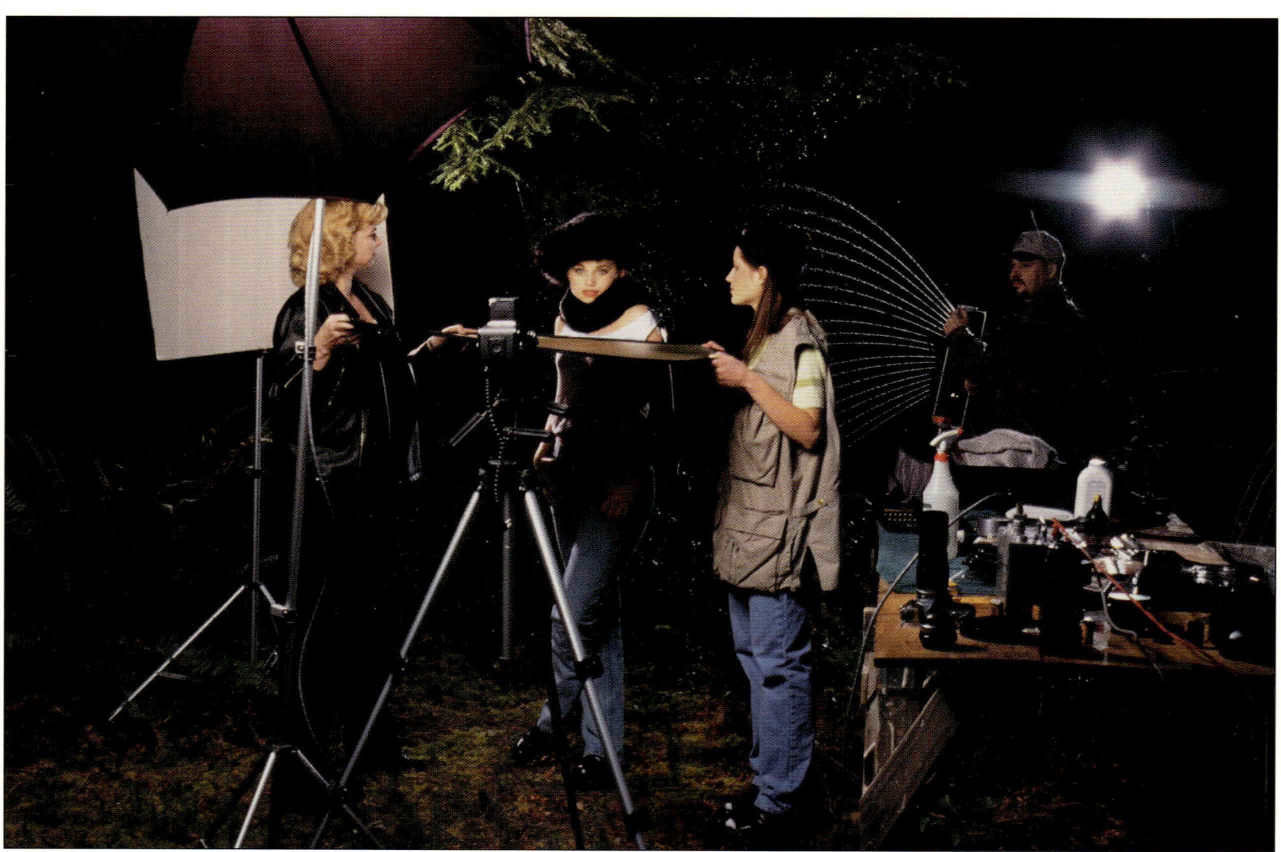

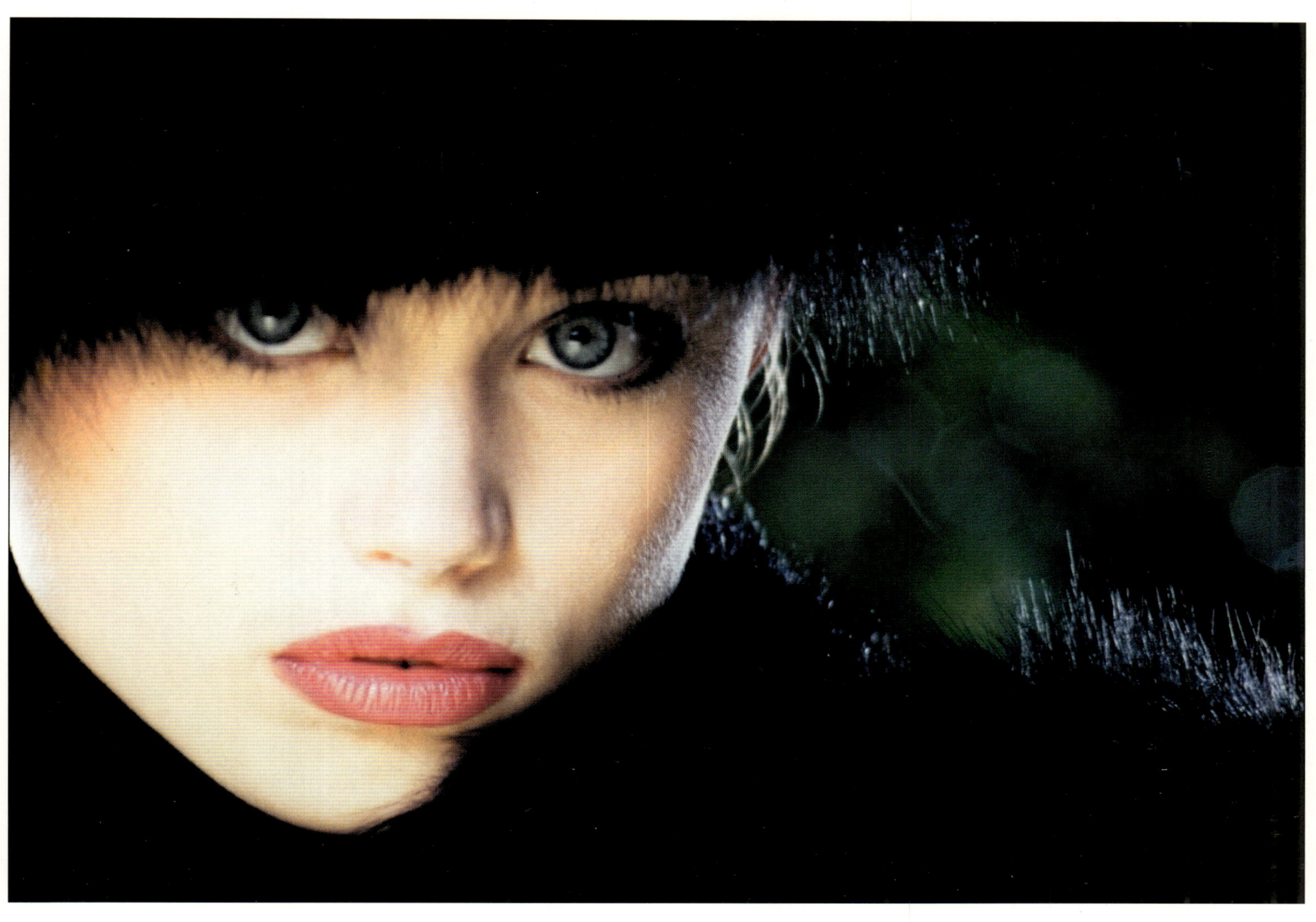

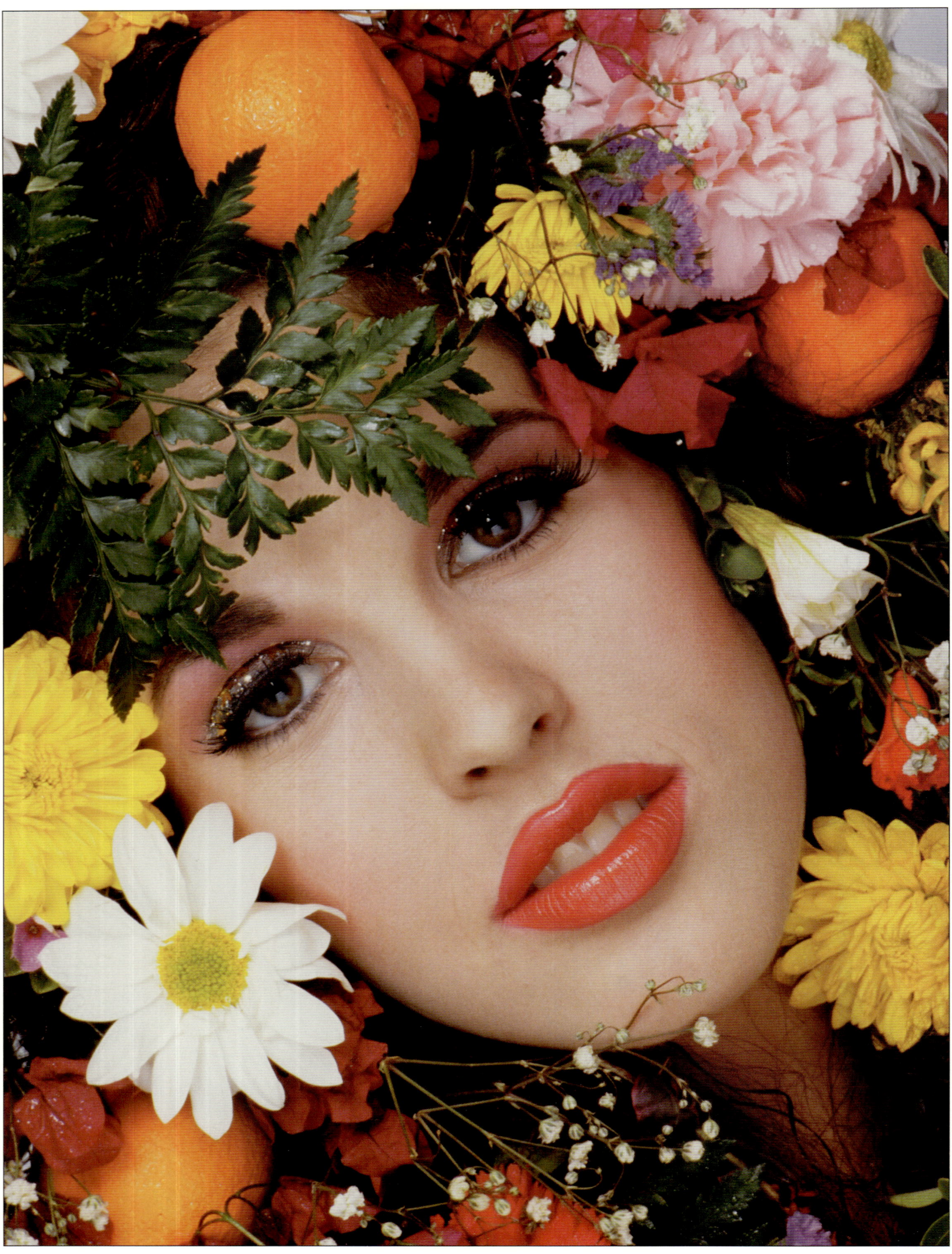

■ Assignment

This image was inspired by a calendar I was working on. A make-up artist was in the studio and saw some of the other images from the book. She said she'd like to do a "fruit salad." The calendar never happened, but the make-up artist, whose work is mostly in film and TV, uses this as an example of some of her more non-traditional work.

■ Posing

We tried a few schemes for arranging the fruit and bright flowers around the model's face. In the end, the only practical solution was to have her lay on her back on white seamless paper. I then shot the photo from a ladder above her.

■ Lighting

An umbrella was placed over the model's head. A reflector placed at her chest level puts a little bit of light under her chin.

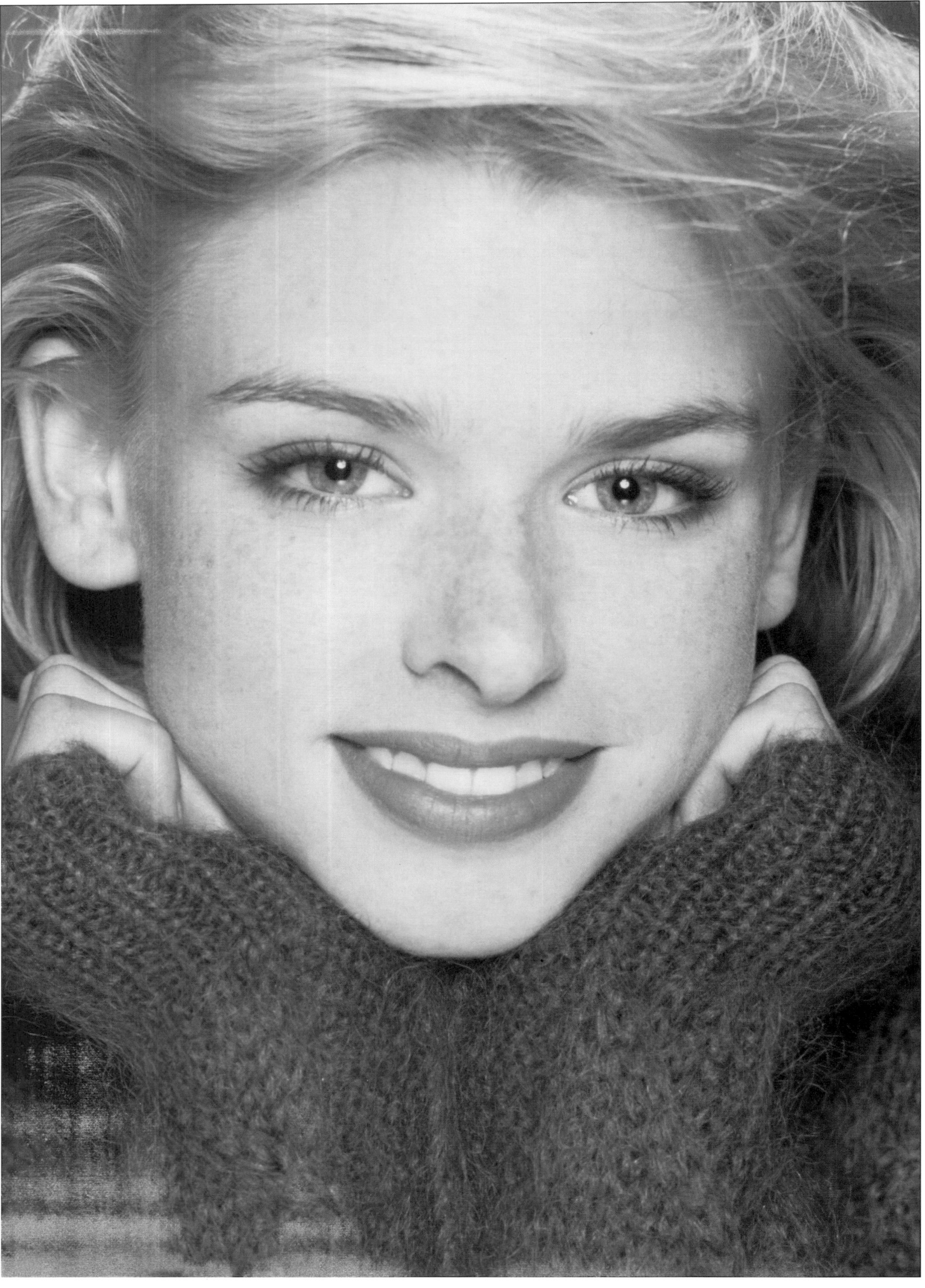

■ Lighting

The lighting set-up for this shot was quite simple. The main light is an umbrella placed as low as I can place it and still be able to shoot under the edge. A hair light was added above and set one stop higher than the main light.

■ Composition

"Clean and fresh" is a look that agents want to see. In a head shot like this, one way to make the skin look smooth and beautiful is to fill the rest of the frame with something that has a lot of texture. Here, the model's skin looks very smooth in contrast with the knit sweater.

■ Posing

In order to draw the viewer's attention directly to the model's face, I had her pose with her head in her hands, but I covered her fingers somewhat with the sweater. Her bare fingers would have drawn attention away from her face. Covered, her hands frame her face nicely.

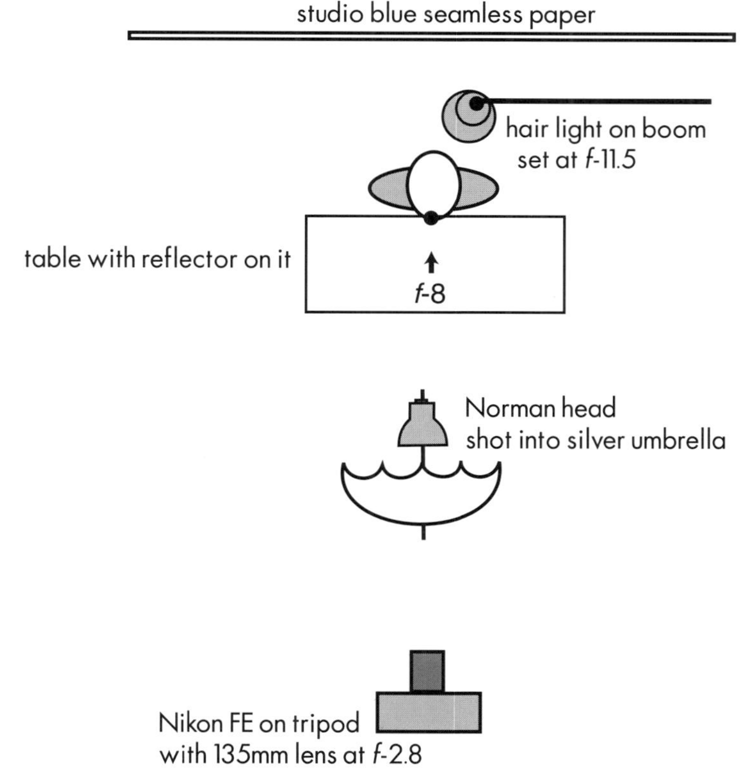

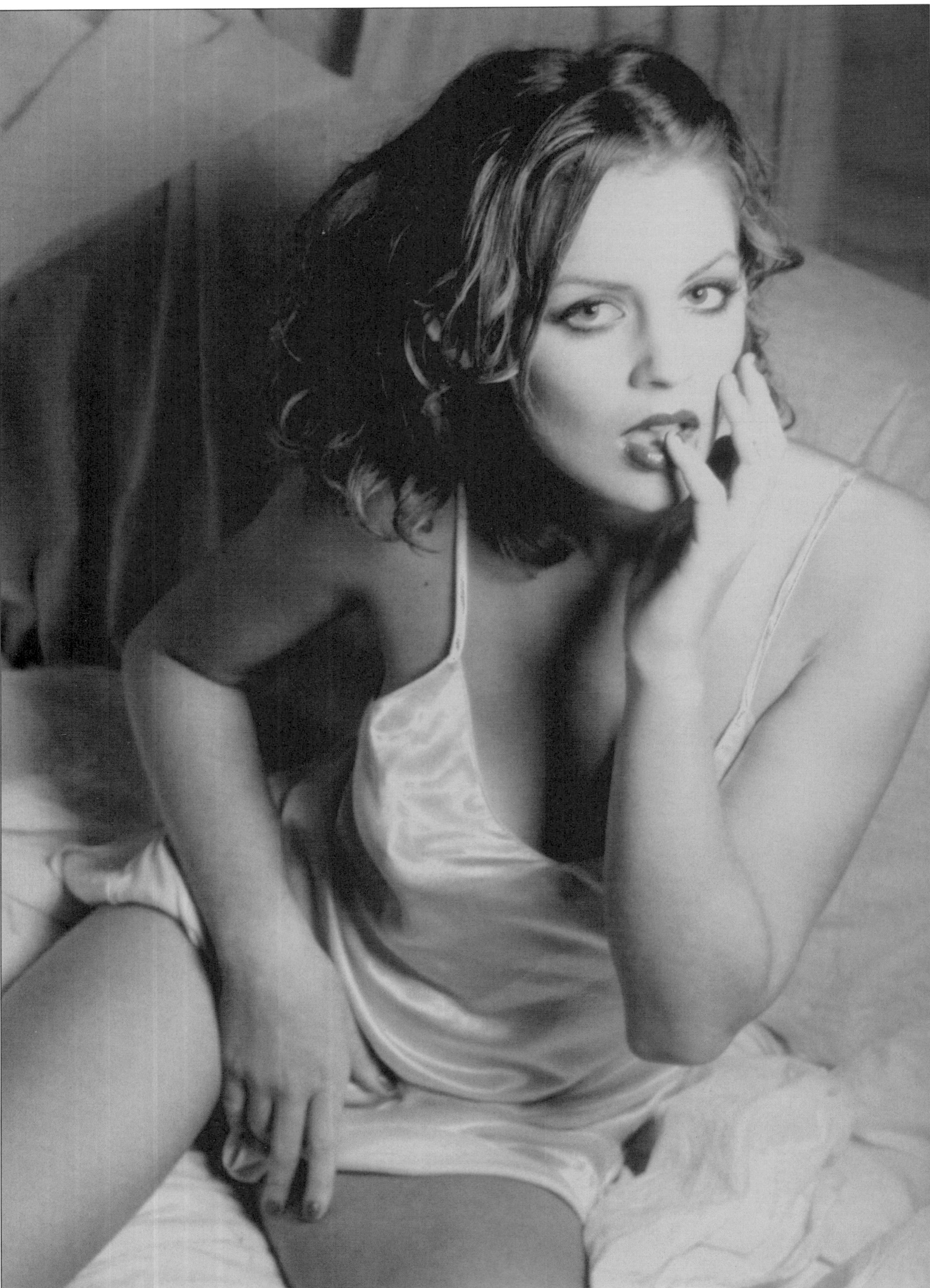

■ Lighting

A tiny soft box was placed to the left of the model.

■ Background

The model was posed sitting on a bunch of white sheets.

■ Photography

The image was shot with the camera elevated to get this interesting perspective.

■ Working with Young Models

I never do nude images with models under 18, even with parental consent. I also never shoot a minor without an adult present, often the mother. Sometimes I even ask the mother to look through the camera and confirm that she thinks the image is appropriate. This model was preparing for the Asian lingerie market, so we took a shot that was sensual, but not explicit.

■ Posing

I get a lot of good ideas from fashion magazines. I read them all to keep up on who's doing what. Especially when working with beginners, it's very helpful to have a list of ideas in mind, since you will need to be able to suggest things. Also, having a lot of ideas at your finger tips is helpful just because people's body proportions vary so widely. A pose that looks one way with one model, may look totally different with another.

It also helps to have new models put together a mock portfolio of tear sheets or ideas where she can see herself replacing the model. Have models create this mock portfolio with the widest range of looks they see themselves fitting into. This mock portfolio can help give you an idea of what kinds of looks and images the modles want to create during the shoot.

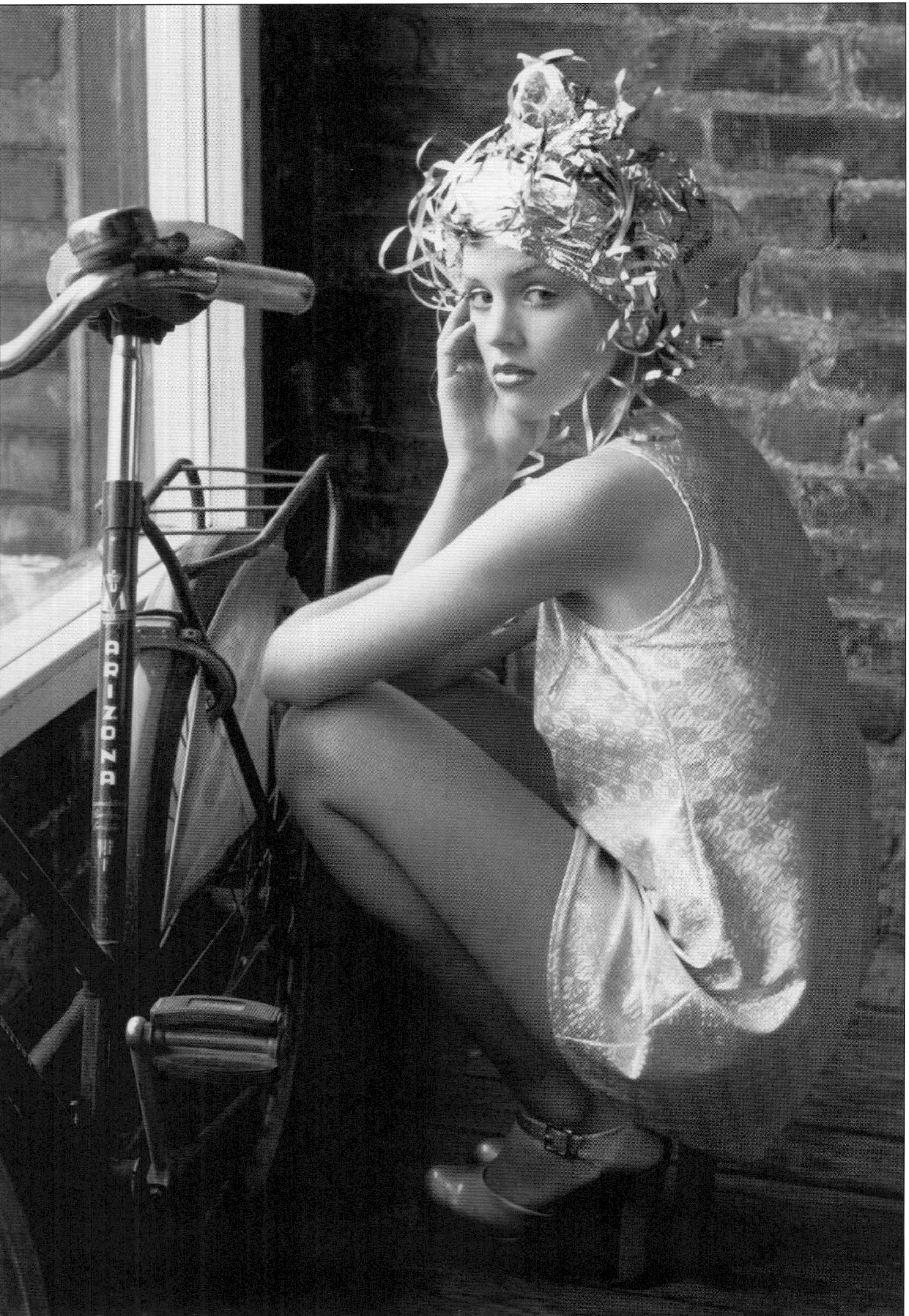

■ Assignment

This image was taken as a promotional shot for a hairdresser.

■ Lighting

The main source of lighting for the photograph comes from the window facing the model. A foam core board was placed 6 inches behind the model. A reflector was also placed on the floor between her and the camera.

■ Photography

I used Elite 200 film for this image in order to get a slightly grainier look.

■ Clothes and Make-up

The hair designer put together this interesting head piece for the model using a skull cap and silver metallic foils. Her dress, shoes and make-up were then coordinated to match the head piece.

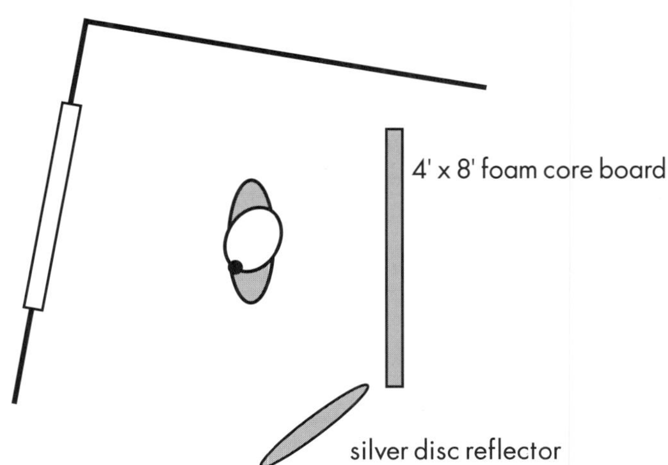

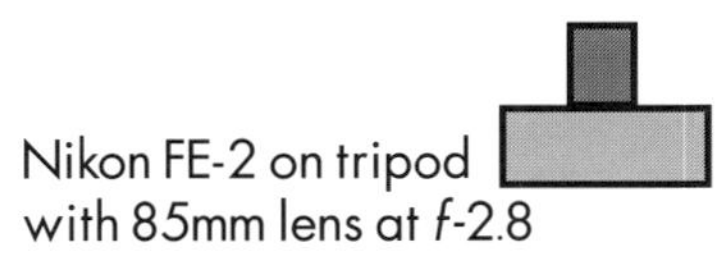

■ Assignment

This photo was used in advertising by a company that sells leather belts.

■ Posing

Two models were used in this shoot. A male model's back is seen on the left side of the frame. The female model is posed above his back with her arm around his waist. The belts were then interwoven with the models' bodies.

■ Photography

A Nikon 85A filter was used to create a warm, romantic light similar to late afternoon sun.

■ Working with Minors

Since the model used in this shot was only 17 years old, I was sure to call the state and confirm that it was permissible to shoot her topless in the studio (even though nothing shows in the photo). It is always advisable to check state law on this matter.

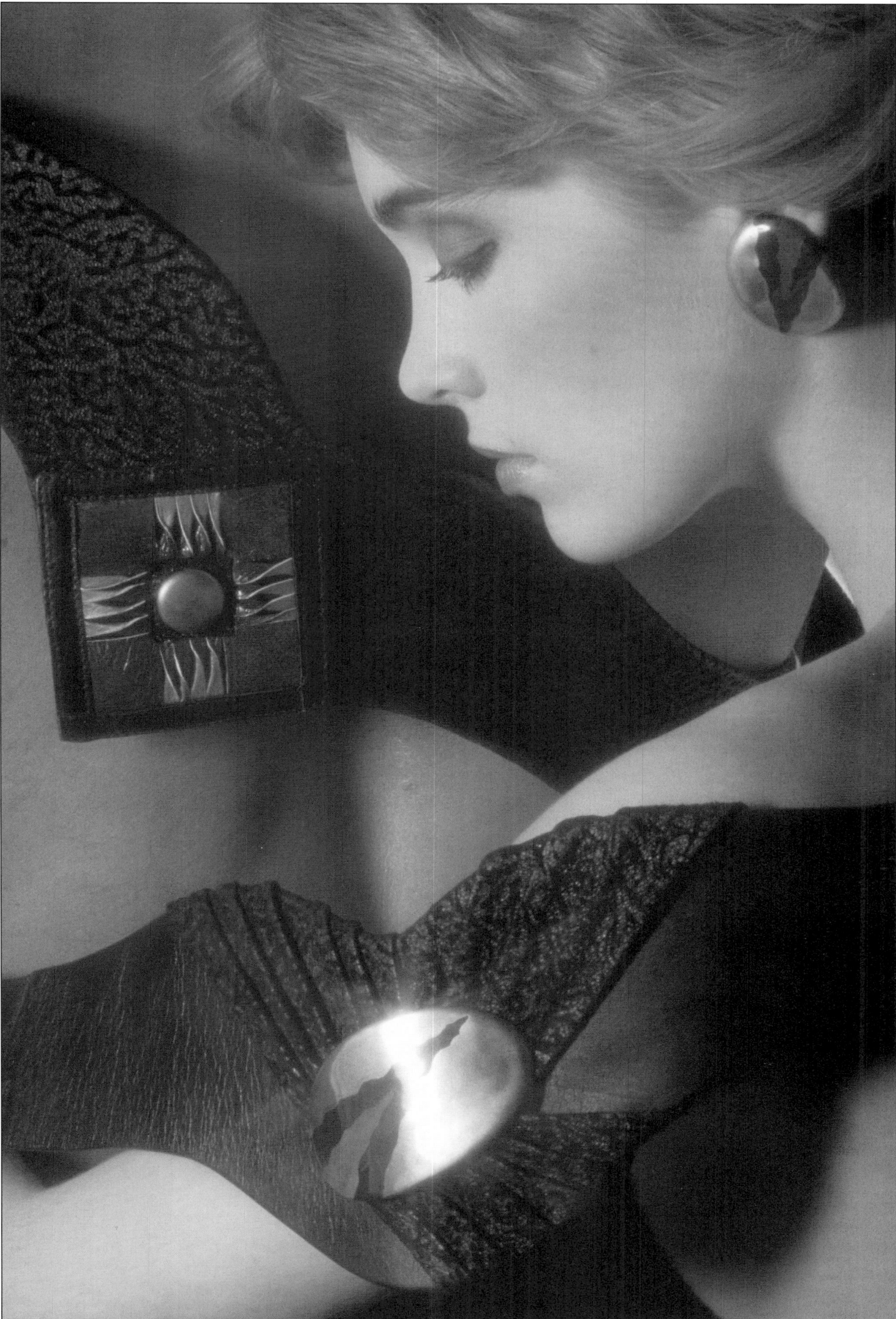

■ Assignment

This photograph was shot for a clothes designer from New Orleans who had put together a line of hats. When I saw them and talked to him, I mentioned that the hats looked like clowns should be wearing them — he said that was exactly the idea! I had to walk the tightrope verbally, so as not to offend the client.

■ Photography

I used a Nikon #1 soft focus filter with an 85A filter on it to create this warm glow.

■ Posing

To fit the mood of the hats, I wanted to do a photo that was full of energy, fun and movement. Therefore I had the model play peek-a-boo, which is how this hand pose came about.

■ Lighting

A soft box was used to the right of the model. She was posed in front of a grey background, and a bare bulb was held close behind her to highlight her shoulders and provide separation from the background.

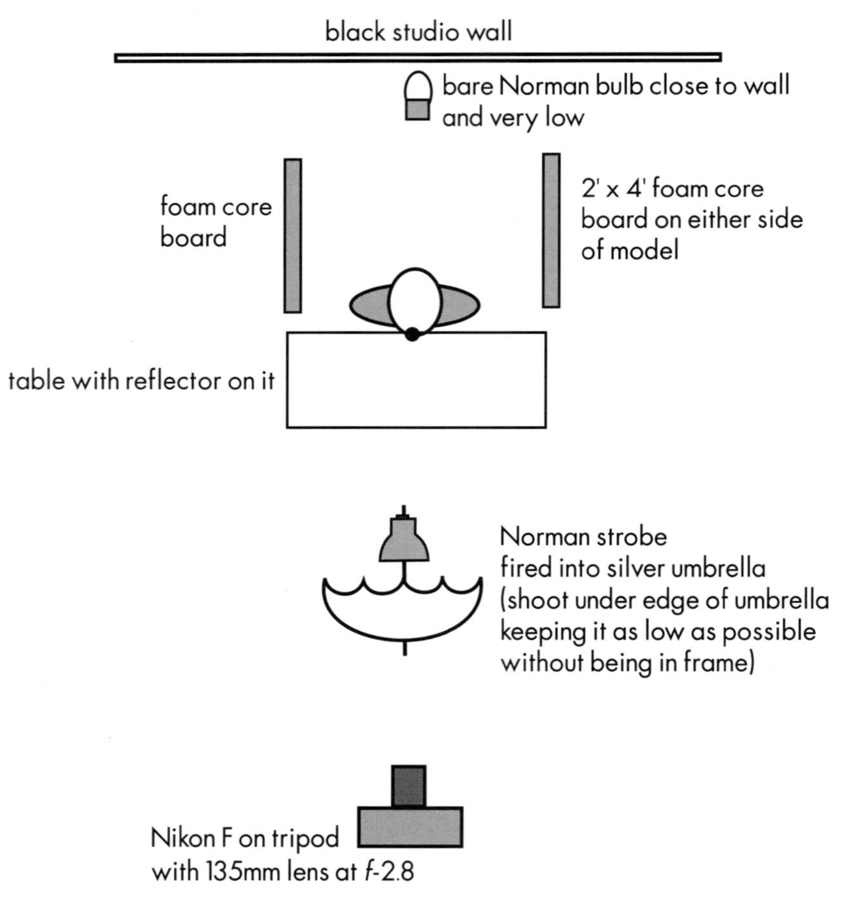

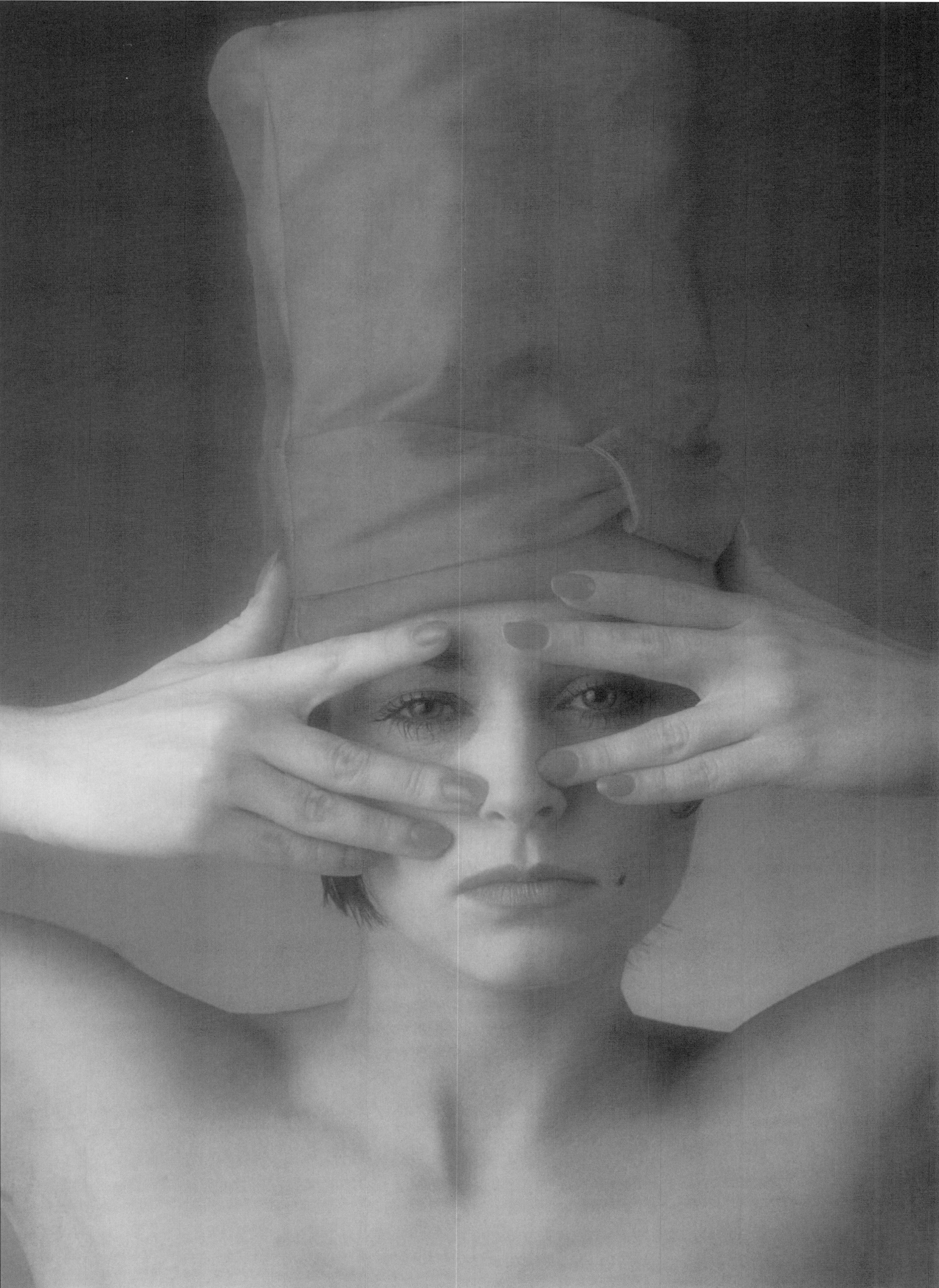

■ Assignment

This image was shot for the model's portfolio.

■ Lighting

The white background is an office wall. I used one umbrella next to the wall and shot under the lip using a Nikon FE camera with a 105mm lens.

■ Posing

Lip posing is often accomplished by having the models say a particular word (such as "hot" or "truly"). Examples of common words for suggesting posing are included below.

Facial Expressions for Fashion and Glamour Posing

Charming	Laughing	Sleeping
Serene	Sensual	Amused
Shy	Curious	Confident
Happy	Excited	Surprised
Flushed	Playful	Angry
Coy	Devilish	Sarcastic
Calm	Cheerful	Alluring

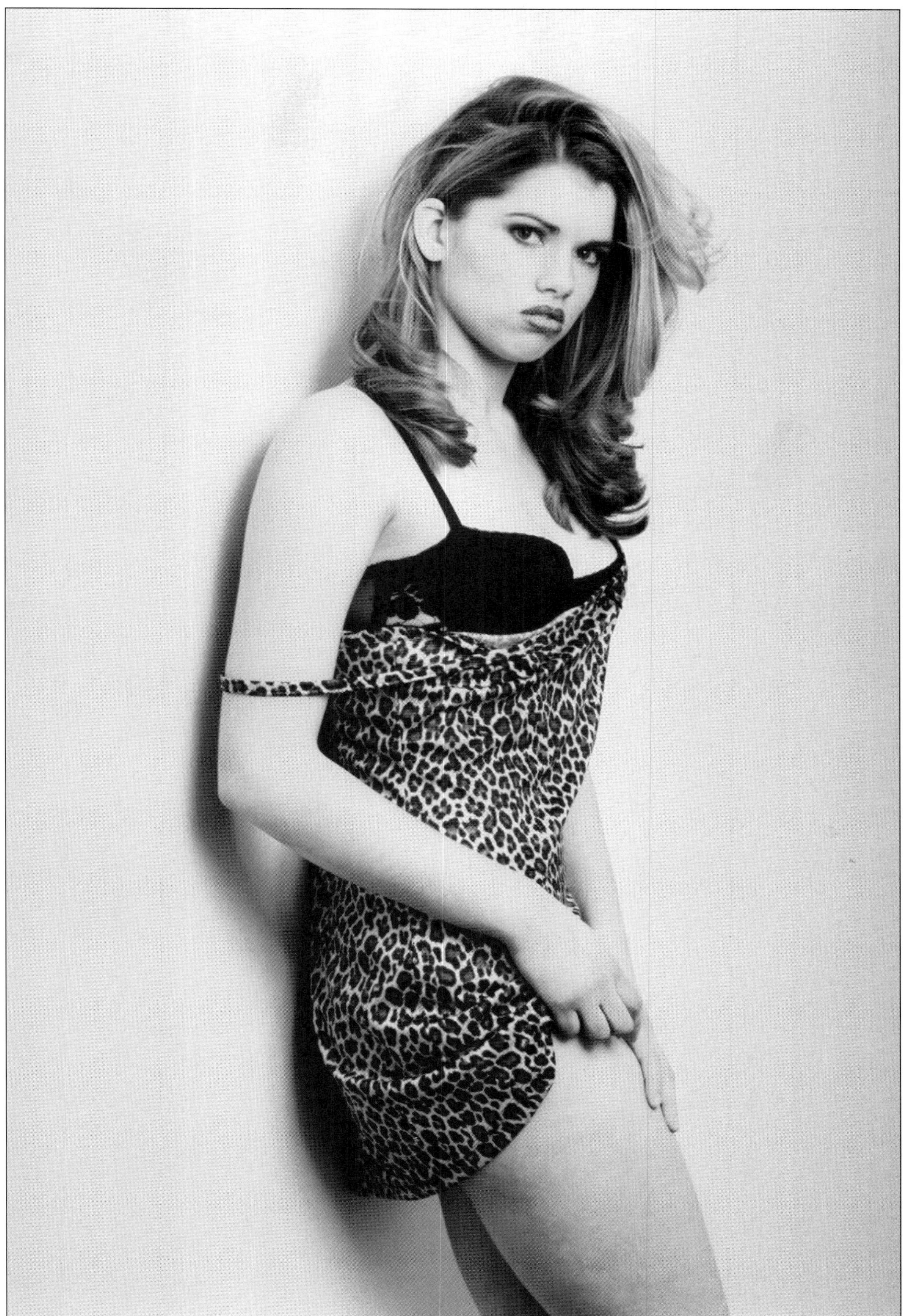

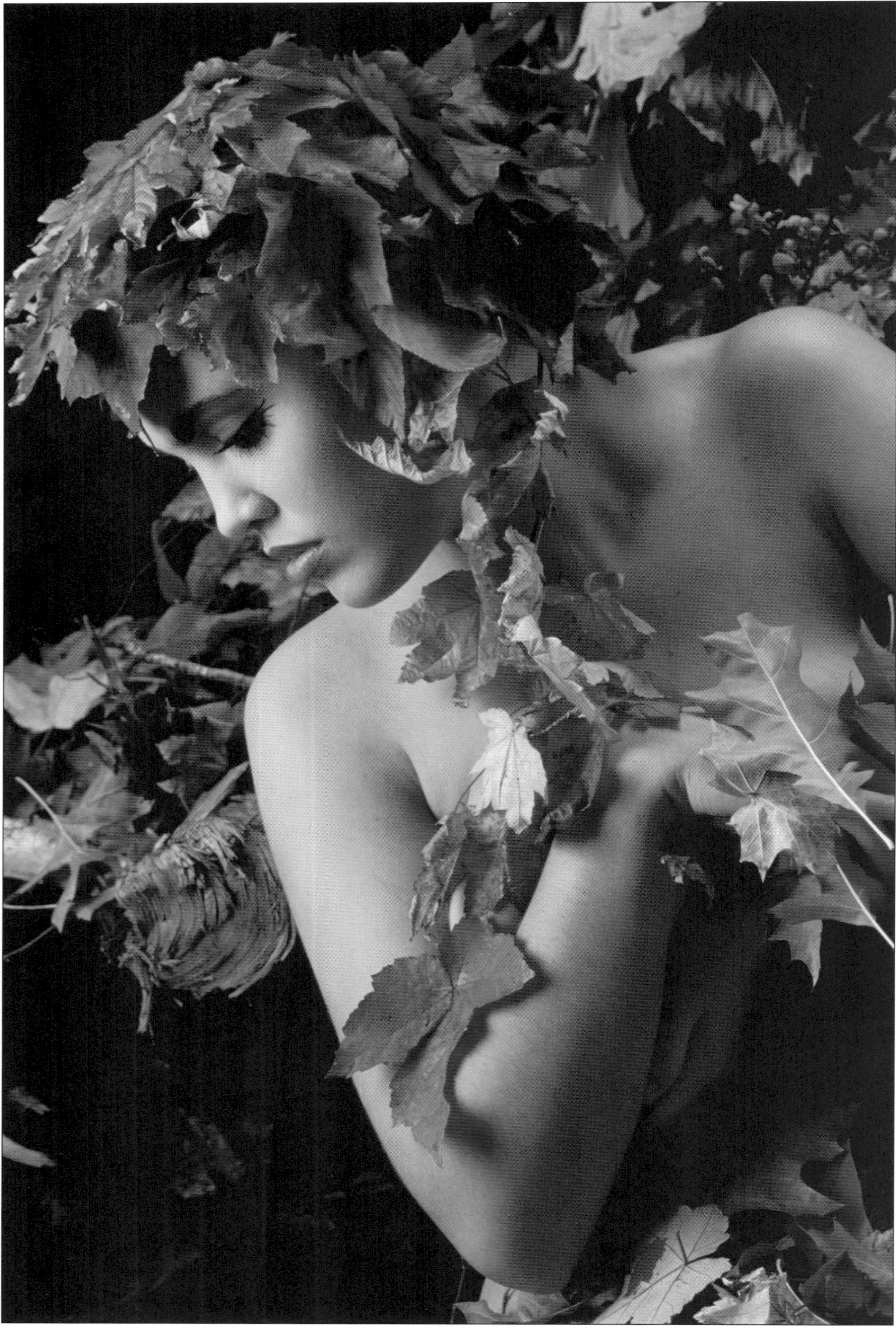

■ Assignment

This image was taken as part of a calendar of fantasy images designed for hairdressers.

■ Background

The background used was black with leaves attached to it.

■ Lighting

A strip softbox was placed to the right of the model. A White Lightning strobe with variable power was coned down to highlight the model's shoulder.

■ Posing

Applying the leaves individually to the model's hair and body was an involved task that took almost five hours to complete. We tried several methods of affixing the leaves, but finally had to pose the model in a seated position with her arms folded and carefully place each leaf on her.

■ Photography

A Nikon FE camera was used with a 105mm lens.

■ Assignment

This image was taken for use by the model in her portfolio.

■ Photography

I used a Nikon FE2 camera on a Bogen tripod with a 300mm lens at f-8.

■ Lighting

The photograph was shot using only available light.

■ Posing

The sun had dropped sufficiently that the model could face it with her eyes open. I placed her about 8 to 10 feet from the wall behind her in order to create a shadow that is strong, but not overpowering. Additionally, the model is posed to show off her flat stomach. To pull her stomach very flat, I had her lift her shoulder and really arch her back. The compression associated with using the 300mm lens disguises the fact that her back is arched.

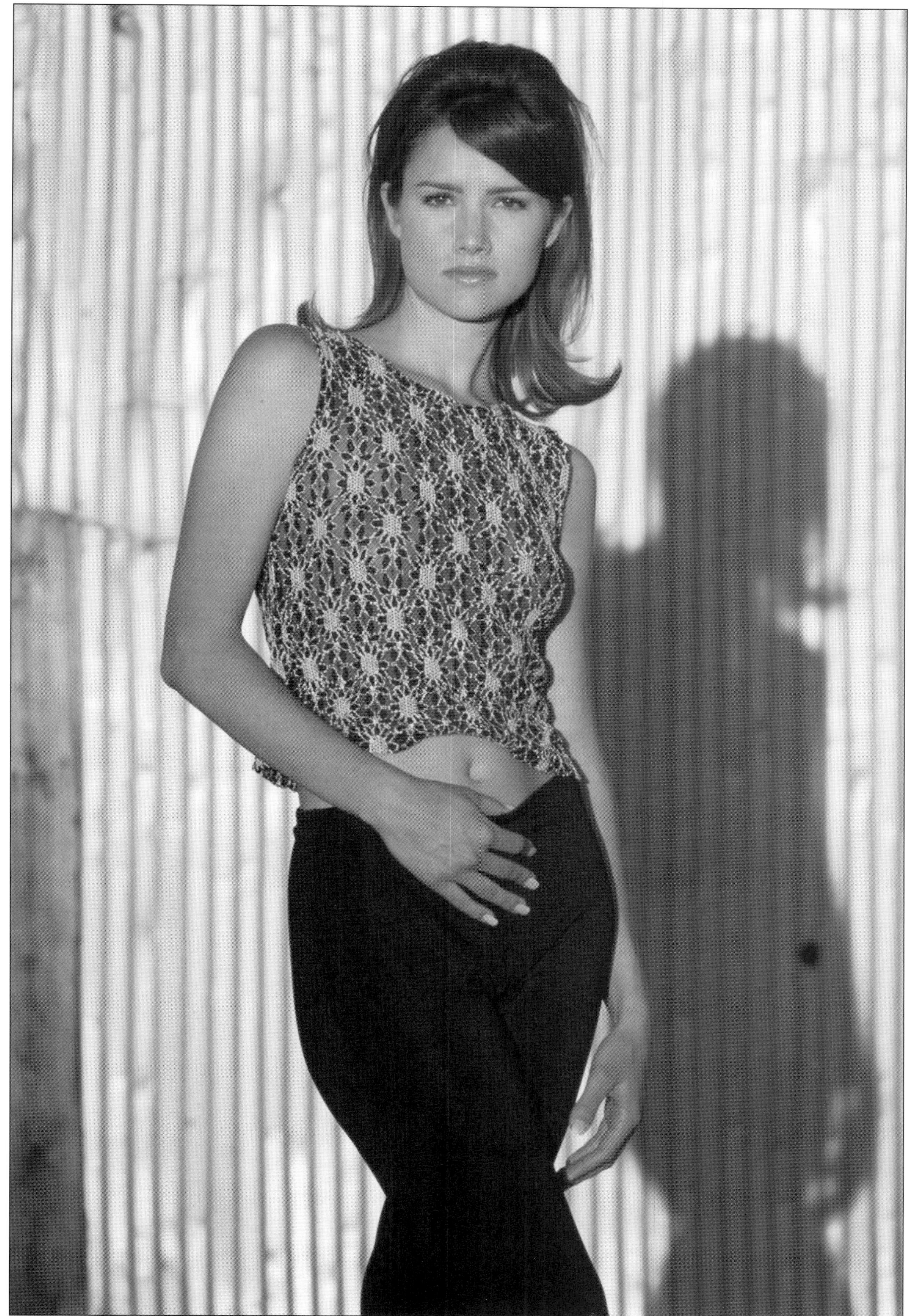

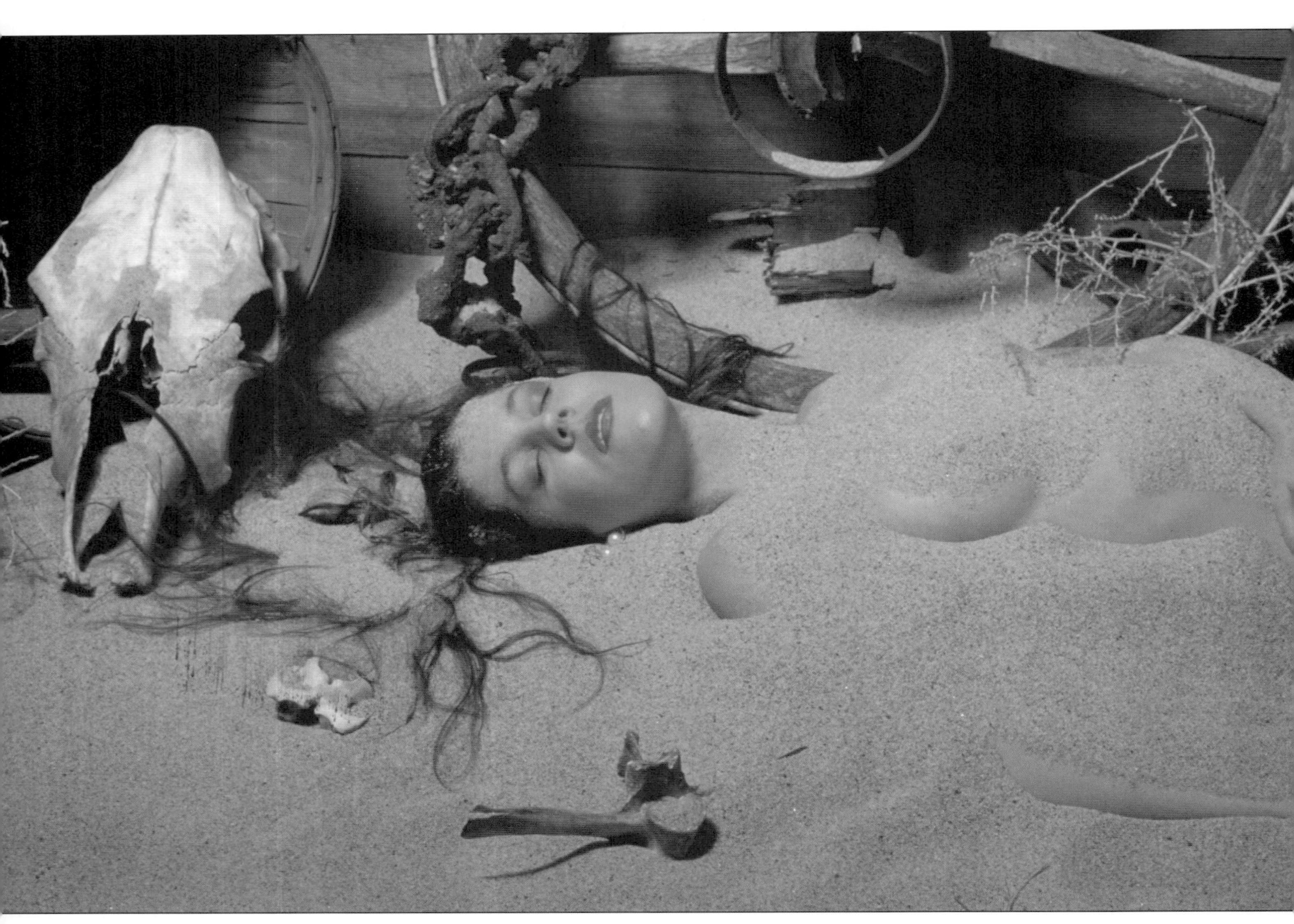

■ Assignment

This image was shot for a calendar.

■ Set-up

To do this shoot, I used 700lbs of sand and a lot of other props which I had on hand from a shoot that had showcased some Southwestern style jewelry.

■ Lighting and Photography

A Norman soft box was placed to the left of the scene. I shot with a Nikon 85A filter. This creates a warm, romantic light. The same filter is used in the photo on page 45, and you can see the similar effect.

■ Inspiration

This image was indirectly inspired by the cover of a National Geographic magazine. The cover featured a photo of a man covered in ice. I shot a photo directly inspired by this (a model in frosty snow and ice), but then started thinking of other ideas in a similar vein. I hit upon using sand instead of ice.

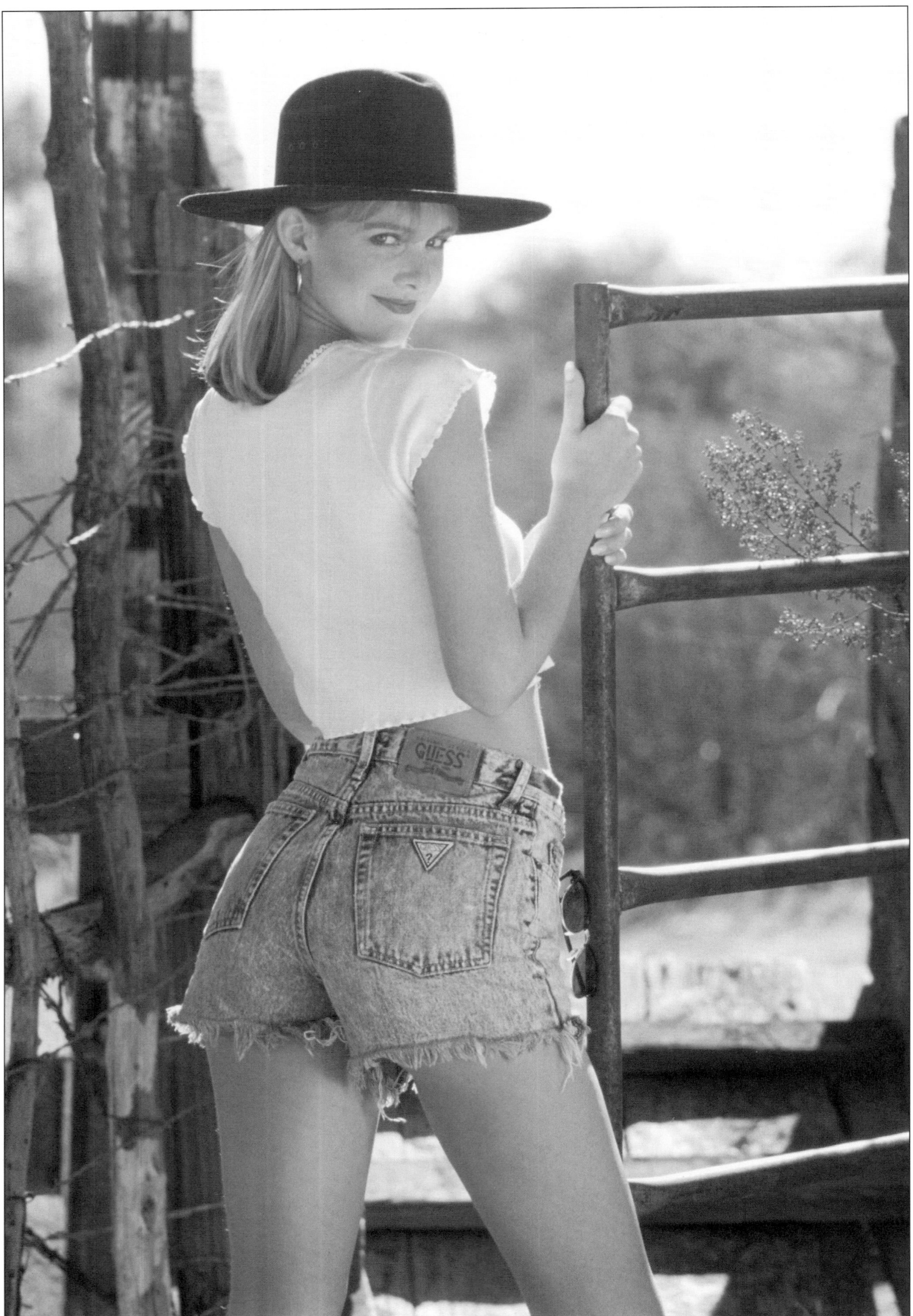

■ Assignment

This image was taken for use in promoting a model's shooting camp.

■ Lighting

The sun was in front of the model's body (as you can see from the highlights on the rail, as well as her hands, shoulder and right breast). A silver reflector was placed to the right of the model to light her face. A 4'x8' piece of plywood that had been painted with highly reflective white paint was held behind the model. The photo was shot from under the edge of the board, which was used as a gobo to block sunlight from the lens and reduce lens flare.

■ Composition

The idea with this image was to use the model's body to fill the gap in the fence. I also tried shooting the image without the model wearing a hat, but it just didn't work. The hat is needed to help fill the negative space at the top of the image.

■ Posing

The pose shows off the model's backside. Having her lift her foot slightly creates a nice line.

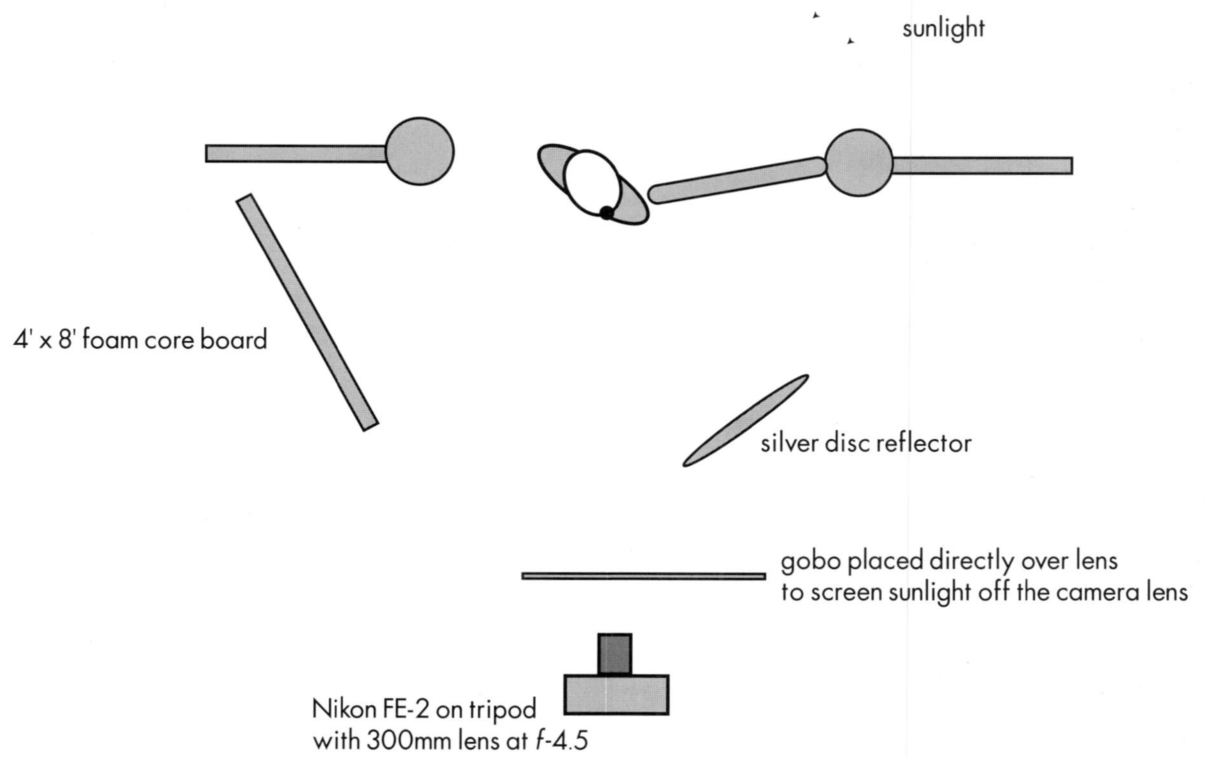

■ Assignment

The image was taken for the model's portfolio. I was going for a look that would be very different than her other photos.

■ Setting

This image was taken under a tree out behind my studio.

■ Posing

The model was posed laying down on a large 4'x8' mirror that was positioned on the ground under the tree where the sun would shine through the branches. The model was wet down for the photo.

■ Lighting

I was trying to create an interesting background with the sun coming through the branches. Unfortunately, the sunlight tended to kick too much light into the camera. The solution was to reposition the model's hair to cover the areas of the mirror where the sun was reflecting too strongly.

■ Photography

Once the scene was set up, the image was shot from a ladder.

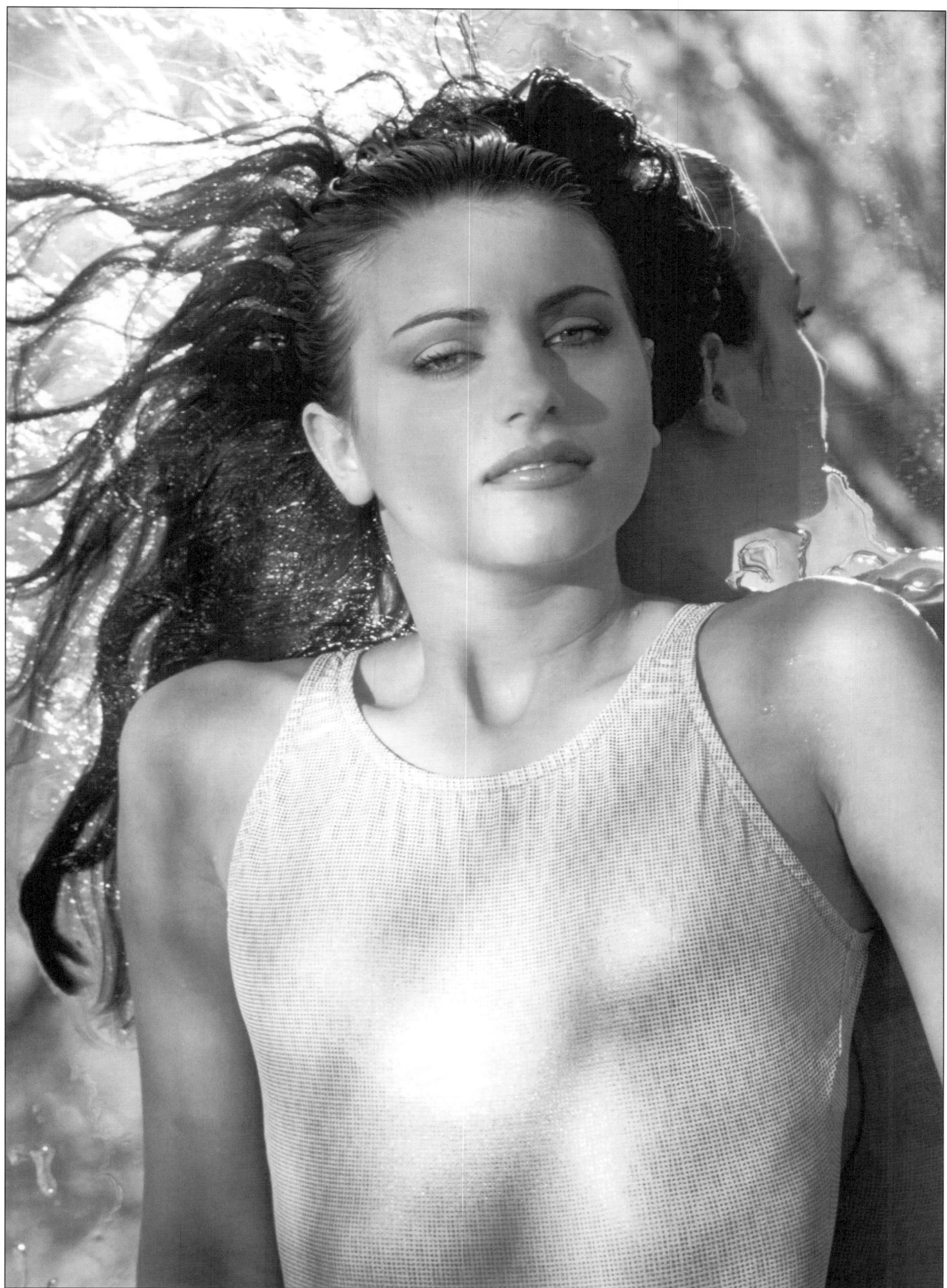

■ Assignment

This topless photograph was one the model just wanted for herself (her boyfriend loved it!).

■ Setting

The photo was shot in the icy cold Sacramento River.

■ Lighting

The lighting used for the image was simply the late day available light.

■ Posing

The model laid in about 6 inches of running water. She was posed with her jeans unzipped and pulled open in order to make her stomach look absolutely flat. A beaded necklace with shells was draped over her upper body to cover her bare breasts.

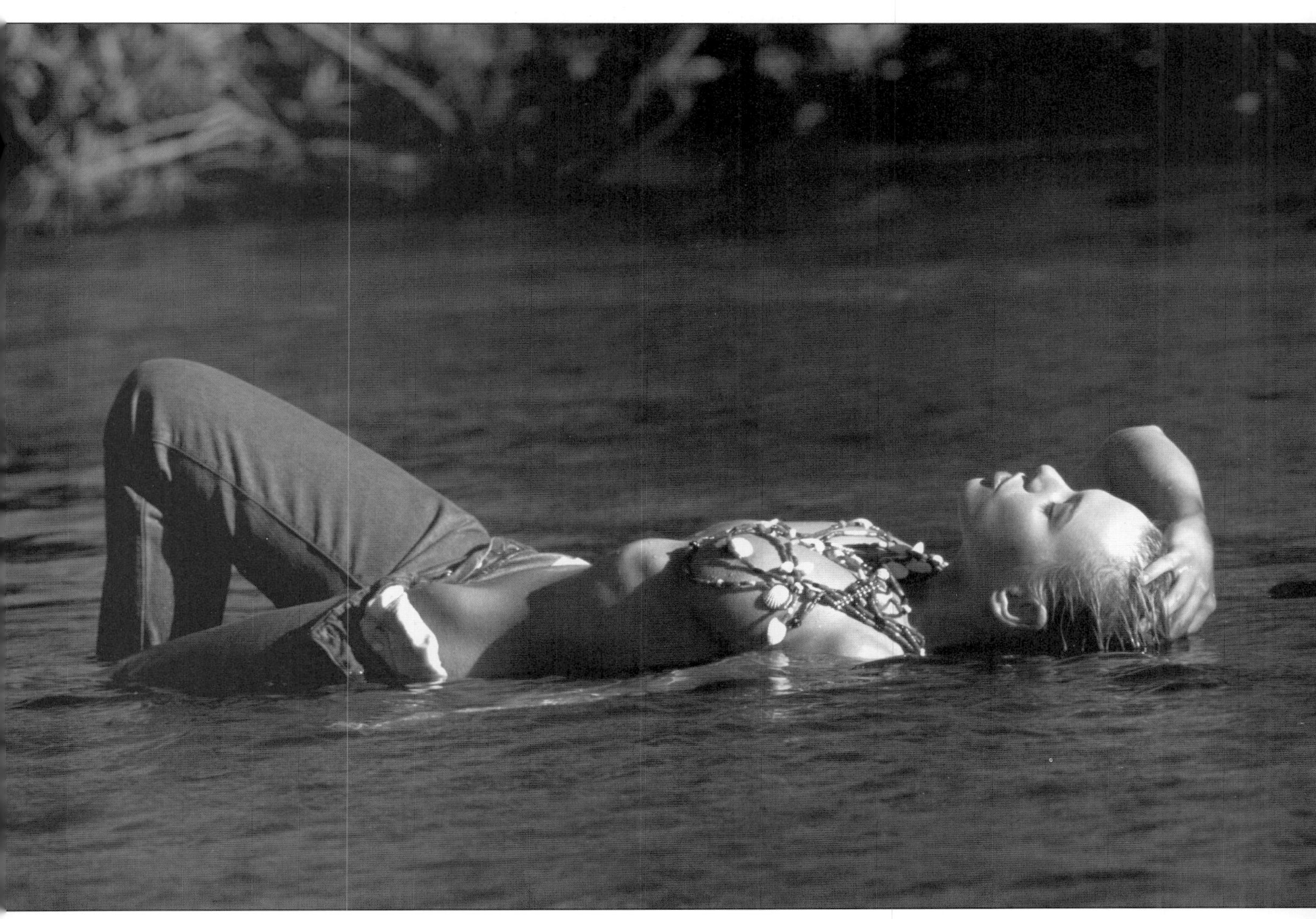

■ Assignment

The image was taken for the model's portfolio.

■ Photography

The camera used was a Nikon FE2 and a 300mm lens. I shot from a low angle to help conceal the fact that the model is a little short. The exposure was 1/8 second at f-5.6.

■ Posing

The model is posed to show off her good proportions, and especially her flat stomach.

■ Composition

I was really going for the reflection on this image. When shooting a reflection, it is especially important to bracket your shots. Also, remember that the reflection will always be darker than the original. This means you will probably want to open up 1 to 1.5 stops.

■ Lighting

The photograph was taken in a breezeway between two buildings. The model was posed close to the opening.

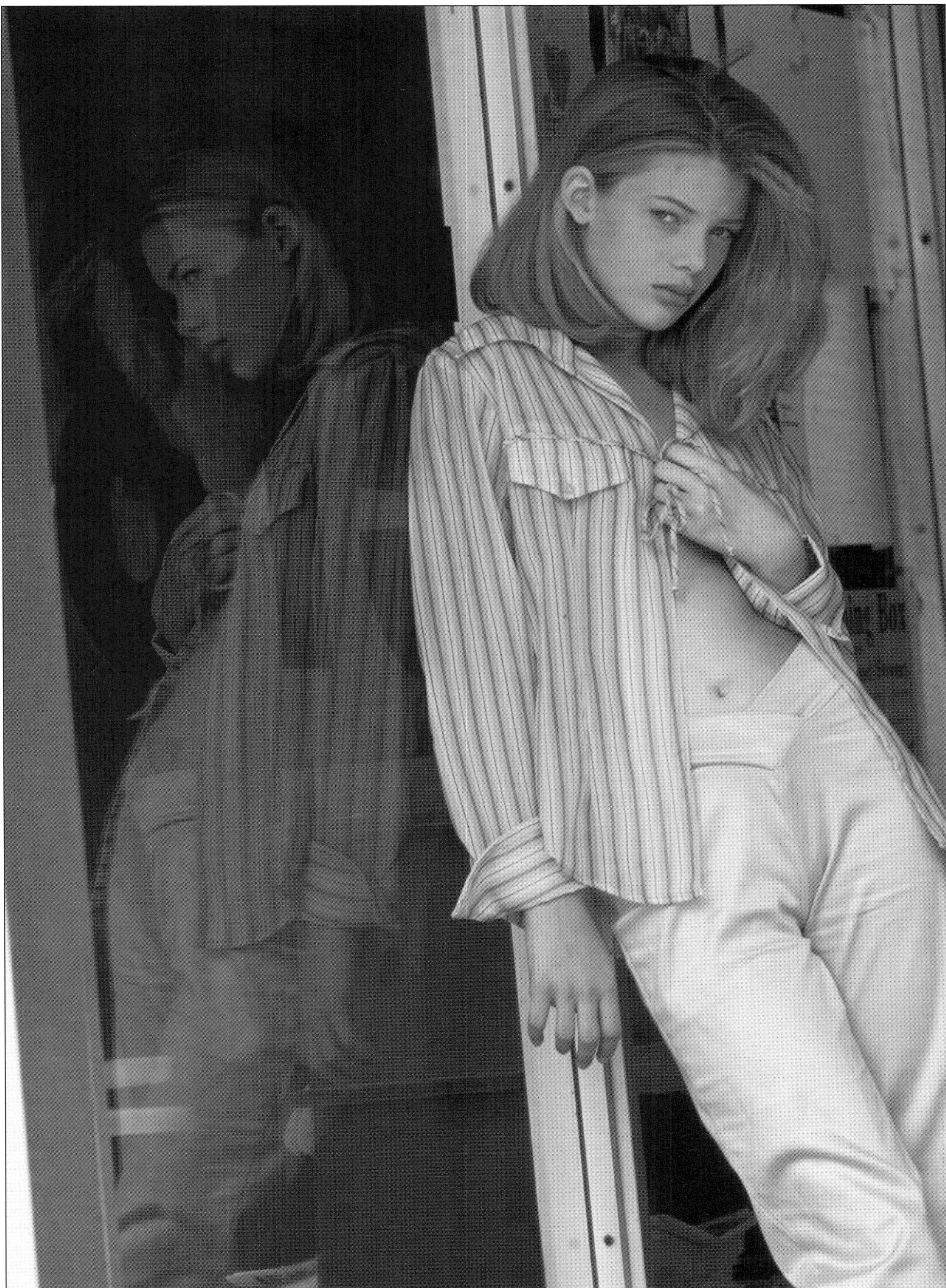
ng Box

■ Assignment

The photograph was taken for the model's portfolio. She had lots of "cute" images in her portfolio, so I wanted to do something with her that would be much stronger.

■ Lighting

The model was posed sitting on a stool in front of white seamless paper. An umbrella was positioned above her.

■ Processing

A black and white image is shown here. The final photograph that was used in the model's book was printed with a brown tone. I made the print about a half stop too dark, then bleached it a lot with a sepia bleach. Once the image was then fixed, it had a nice brown tone. If you go too far with the bleach, you can always darken it up by using a sepia toner.

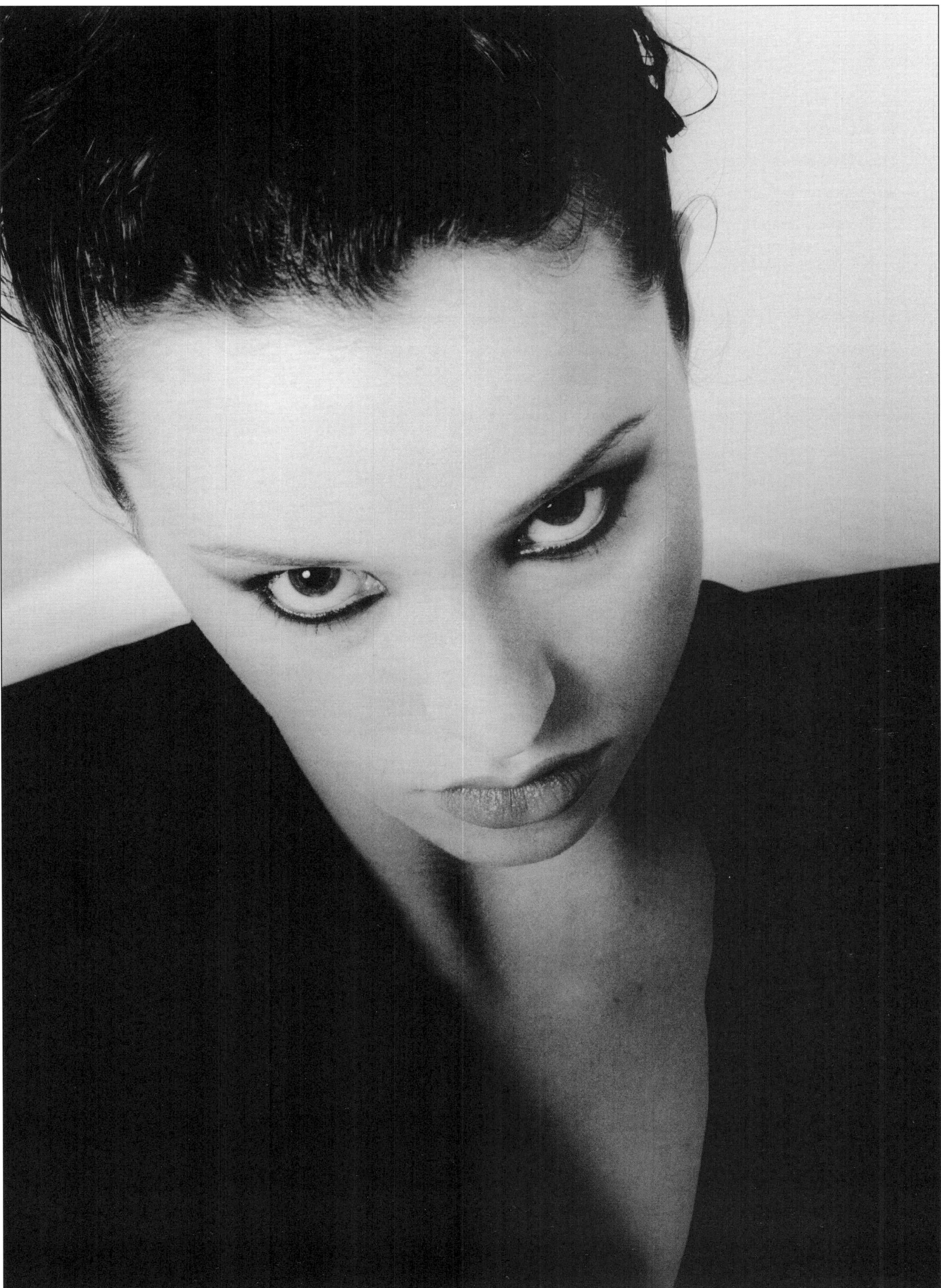

■ Assignment

This image was taken for a member of the Arizona Bikini Team, who wanted a photograph to show off her sensuality and glamour.

■ Photography

Shooting with a 300mm lens, I tried to get the camera on the model's eye level. Shooting down on the model would have destroyed the impact of the image.

■ Posing

The pose is sexy, yet not too revealing. The model was covered in sand for the shoot.

■ Lighting

A tree was to the right of the model and she was posed in the shadow beneath it. A silver reflector was positioned in front of her and causes the highlights in her eyes.

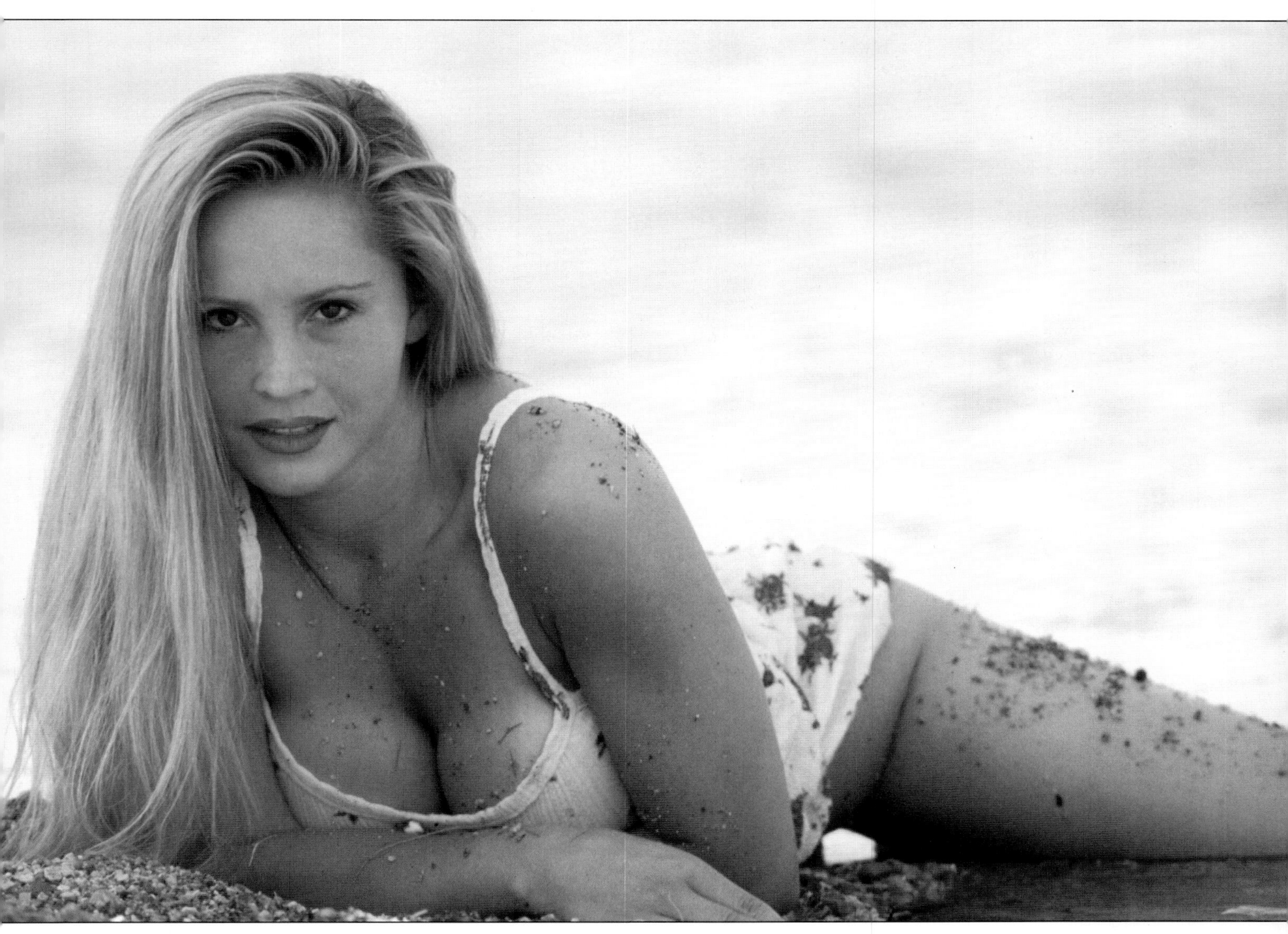

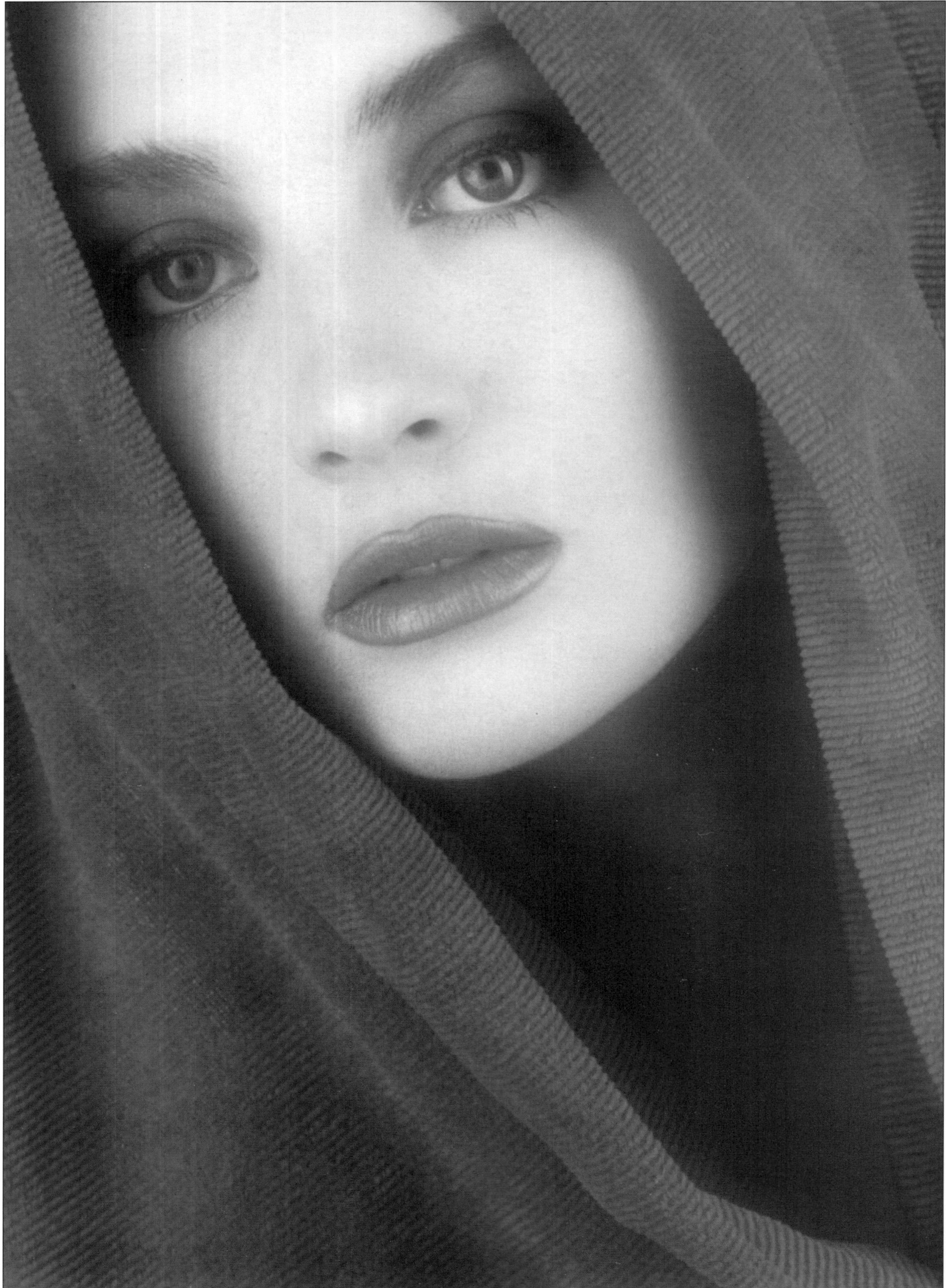

■ Assignment

This image was for the model's portfolio.

■ Lighting

A soft box was placed to the left of the model. A foam core board was positioned close to her left shoulder. The combination of these two lights accounts for the two catch lights in her eyes.

■ Photography

A Nikon #1 soft focus filter was used to soften the image.

■ Posing

We were having a little hair problem. Since I really wanted to emphasize the model's beautiful face, I covered her head with a piece of heavy velour. This makes her face the focal point of the image. Her make-up was also adjusted to compliment the tones of the fabric.

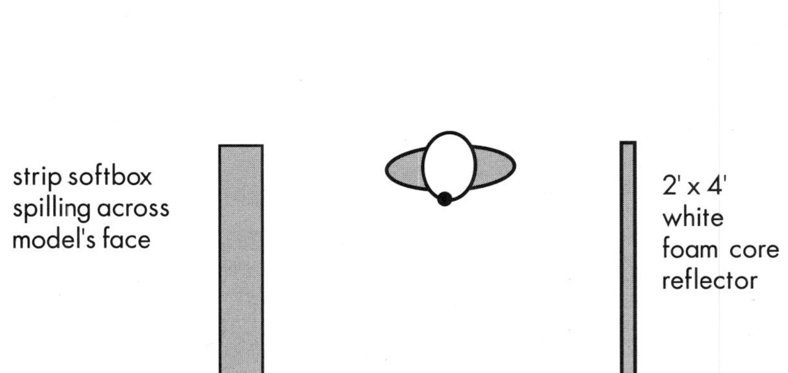

■ Assignment

The image was for the model's portfolio.

■ Posing

This is another photograph where the posing was influenced by a need to compensate for imperfect hair or make-up or clothes, etc.. On top of this, we were running out of light. For this reason I decided to do some body shots. This pose shows off the model's body, especially her legs. Her legs are stretched out to make them look even longer and leaner.

■ Setting

The photo was shot in a drainage ditch lined with stones. I really liked the contrast between the model's skin and the rocks, as well as the light.

■ Lighting

The sun was just about to drop below the horizon when we were shooting.

■ Photography

I shot the photograph from bottom of the ditch up toward the model. I used a 200mm lens.

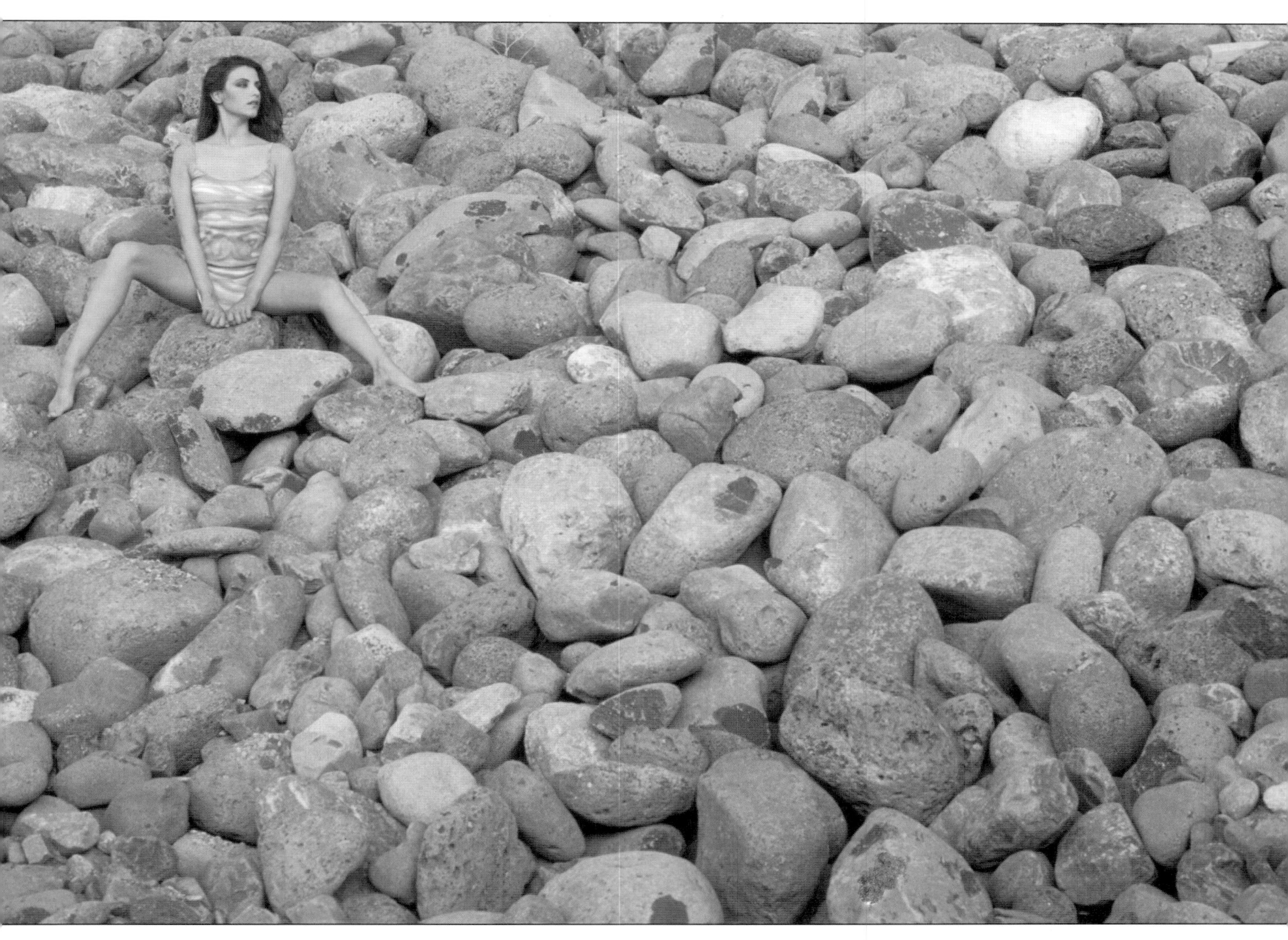

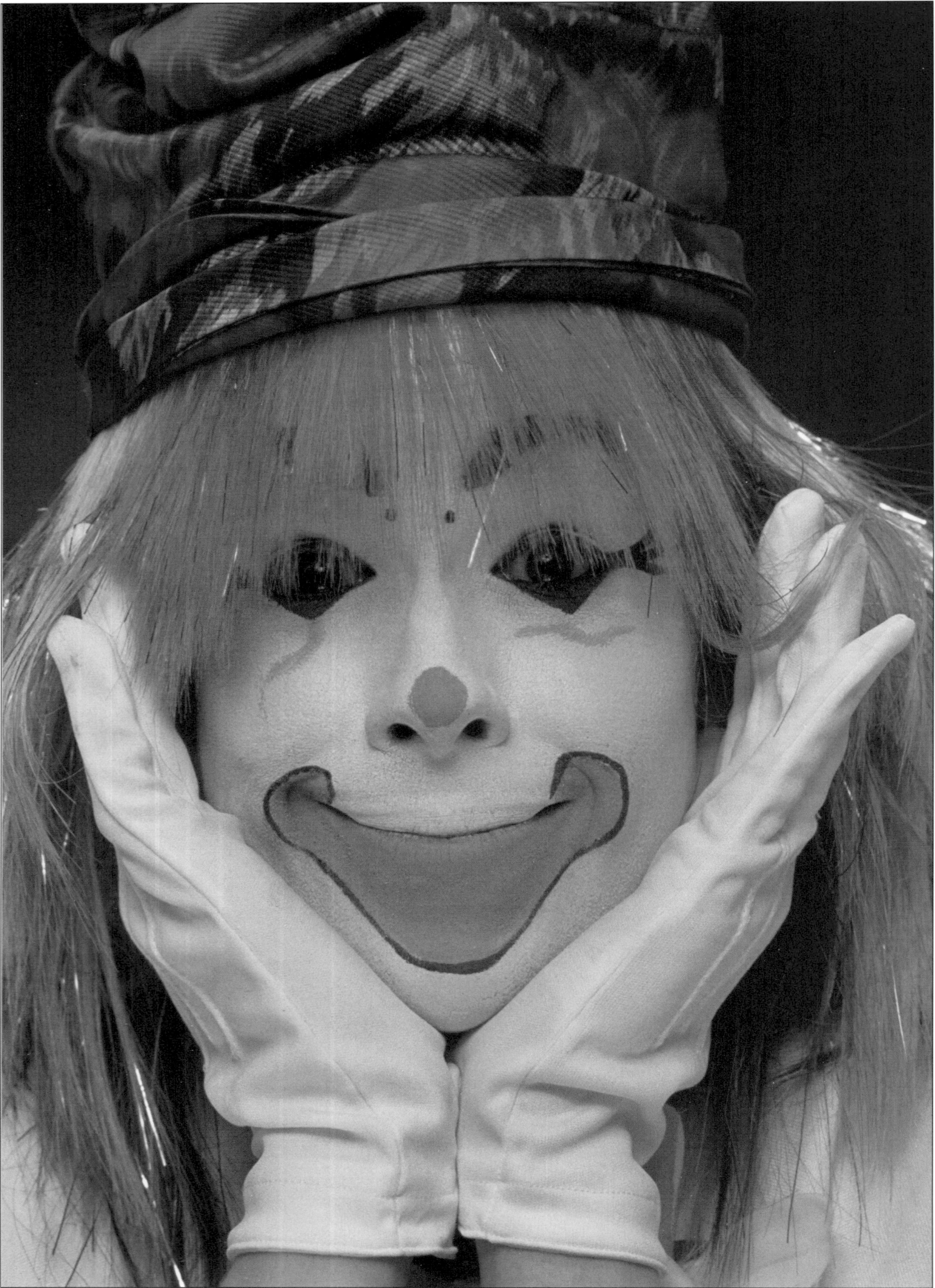

■ Assignment

Like the photograph on page 47, this photograph features a hat made by a New Orleans designer. I had a friend in the studio who is actually a professional clown. We were taking some photographs for her to use on her business cards, but we also took some photos with the designer's hats.

■ Lighting

The model was posed in front of a black wall with a soft box straight overhead.

■ Posing

I sat the model at a drafting table. This is something I use frequently for head shots, since the tilting table provides a great place to position a reflector and a place for the model to put her hands (or in this case, prop her elbows). The lighting and pose make this a soft, rather than overpowering, image that really shows off her smile.

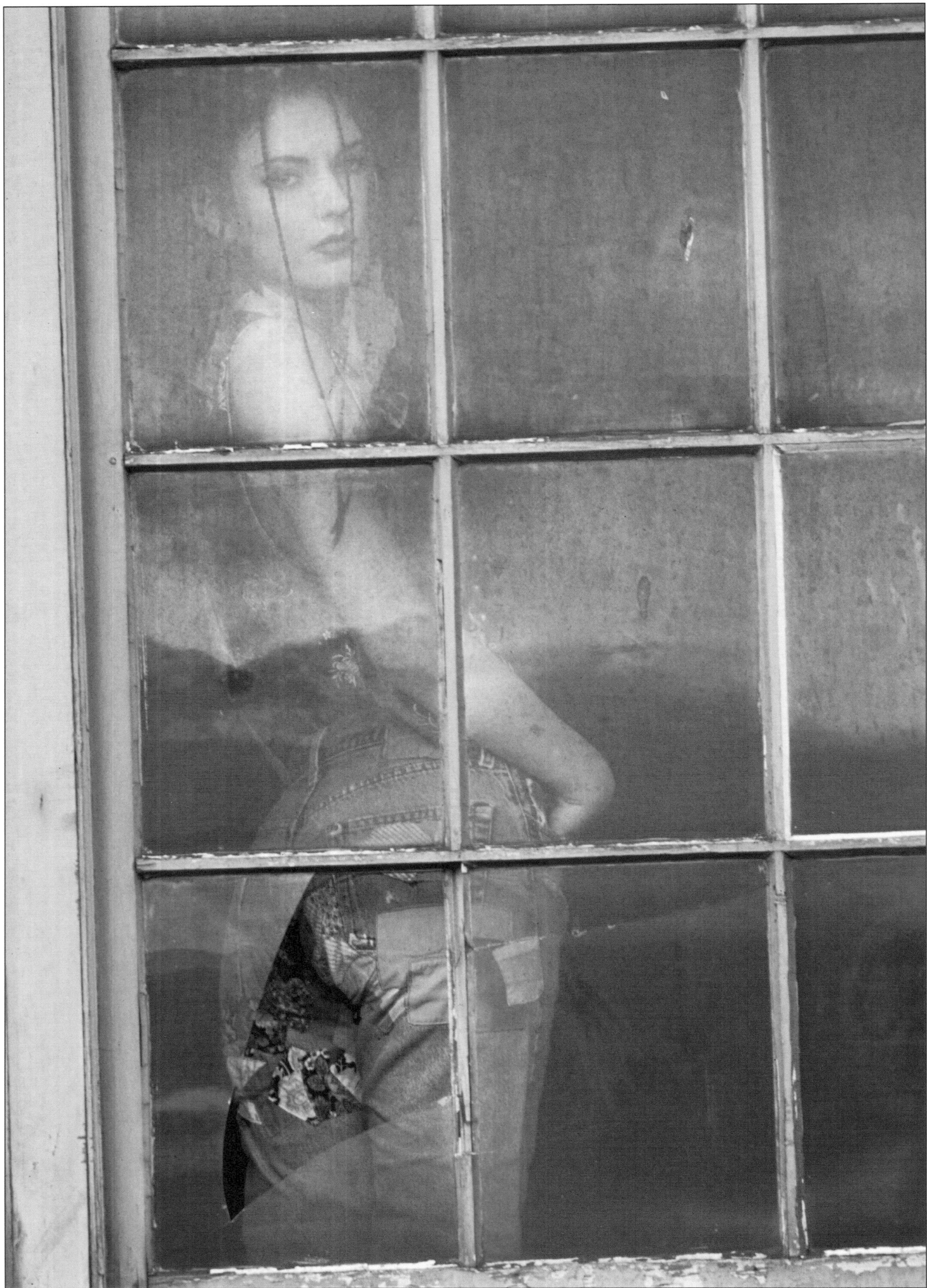

■ Assignment

This photograph was taken for a designer who makes silk vests, then takes remnants of the fabric to dress up your jeans and create a coordinated outfit. The focus of this photo was the jeans.

■ Setting

The phot was shot at an old building with broken windows near my studio.

■ Posing

The model was positioned in front of a broken window with the patched part of her jeans showing through the broken glass. She had to pose on a stack of bricks in order to get her at the right level.

■ Lighting

Only natural light was used for the image. The window faced out onto an alley so natural shadows created a nice even light on the window. I was sure to bracket the image well in order to make sure I got a good exposure.

■ Assignment

The image was taken for a designer who makes jackets.

■ Photography

Since this was a shot to be used for commercial purposes by the designer, I shot it with a medium format camera, a Mamiya RB67. It was raining during the shoot, and I had to keep the camera under an umbrella.

■ Composition

The models were posed in a way that mimics the curve of the stacks in the background. The wet roof above a hair salon was highly reflective and added to the pose.

■ Hair

Because this photo was intended to show off the coats, it was necessary to downplay the models somewhat. One model was blonde and the other brunette, so the hairstylist fitted two skull caps with gold lame. The identical headwear makes the models look much more uniform and ensures that they don't distract your attention from the clothes.

■ Printing

To get this great reflection, when printing I burned in the area around where the model's are standing.

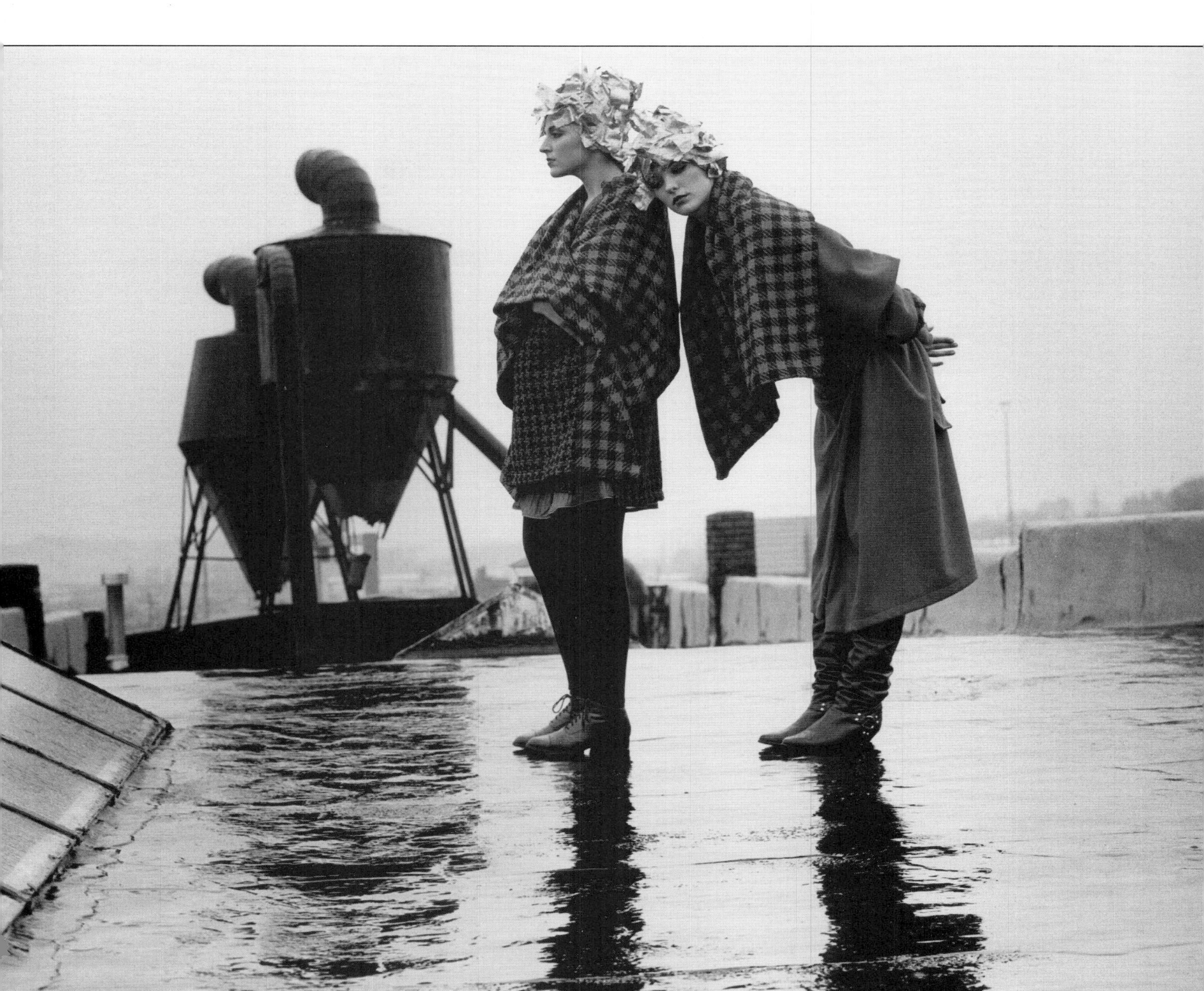

■ Inspiration

I took this image as the result of a conversation I had in which I pointed out that a really great model doesn't needy fancy or expensive clothes to look absolutely beautiful. The image has been a useful one in recruiting models, since girls I approach about photographing often feel it could be a problem that they don't have a lot of expensive designer clothes to wear for a shoot. After all, a good model can wear rags!

■ Setting and Lighting

The photograph was shot outside my studio. It was about 8 o'clock in the evening and the sun was dropping and the model was in shadow.

■ Finding Models

I always have my eyes open for potential models; whether I'm out for breakfast, at the theater or in the mall, I'm always looking. When I see someone I would like to work with, I approach her with a business card and invite her to come with an escort to my studio to look through my portfolio. When I started out, only about 10% of the people I approached would call back. Now that my reputation has grown, almost 90% of the people I approach will eventually come in to talk about doing photographs.

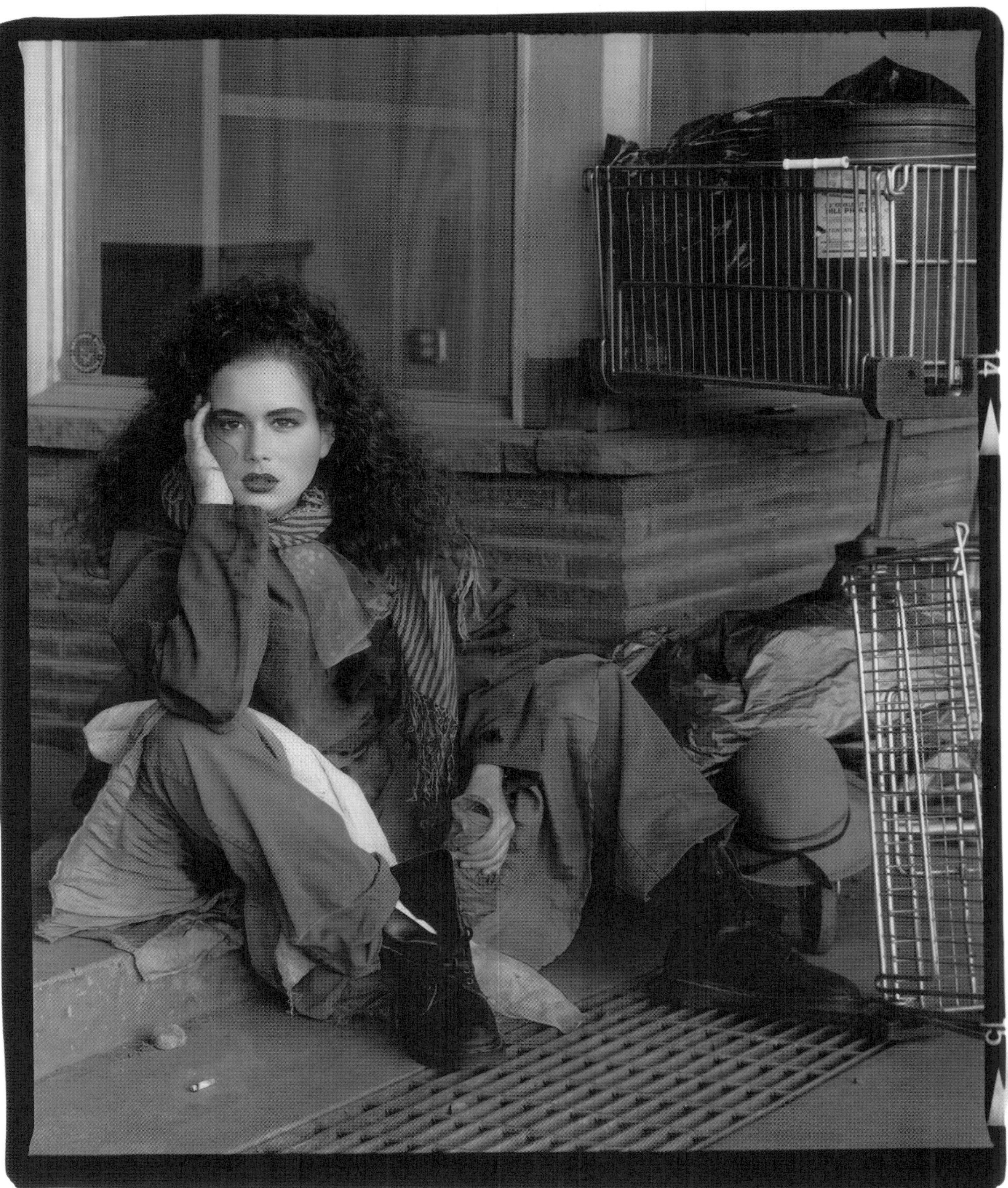

■ Assignment

This image was shot for a hairdresser in Palm Springs.

■ Posing

I wanted to do a really unique image, so I selected a site with this fence and the windmills in the background. Using rubber bands, the model's hair was tied up to the fence.

■ Lighting

A mirror was positioned to light only her face and downplay her body. I then metered the shot for the model's face.

■ Composition

The model's knees and face create a triangle which, combined with the lighting, draws the viewer's eye to the model's face and hair.

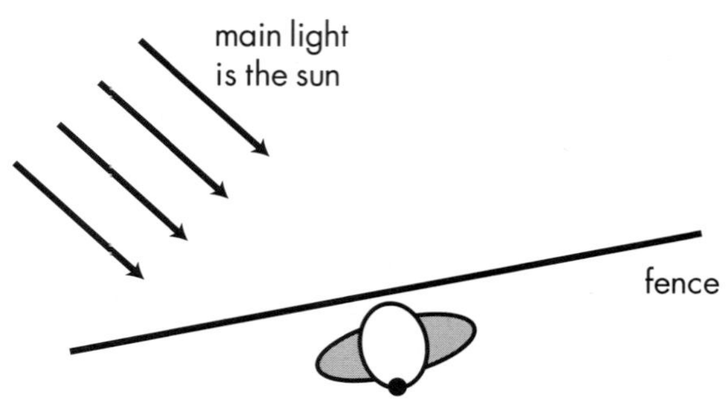

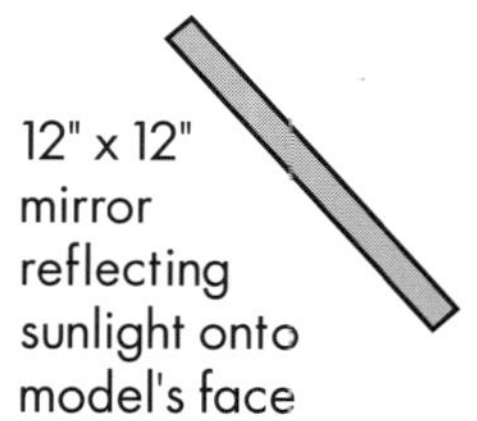

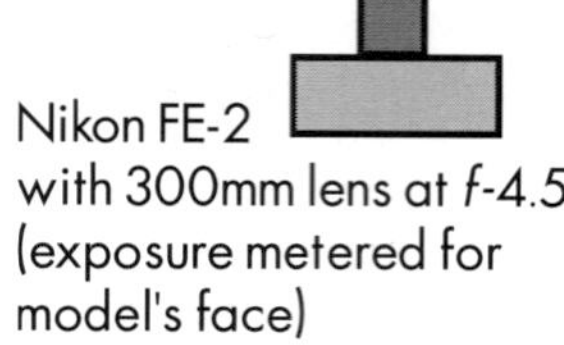

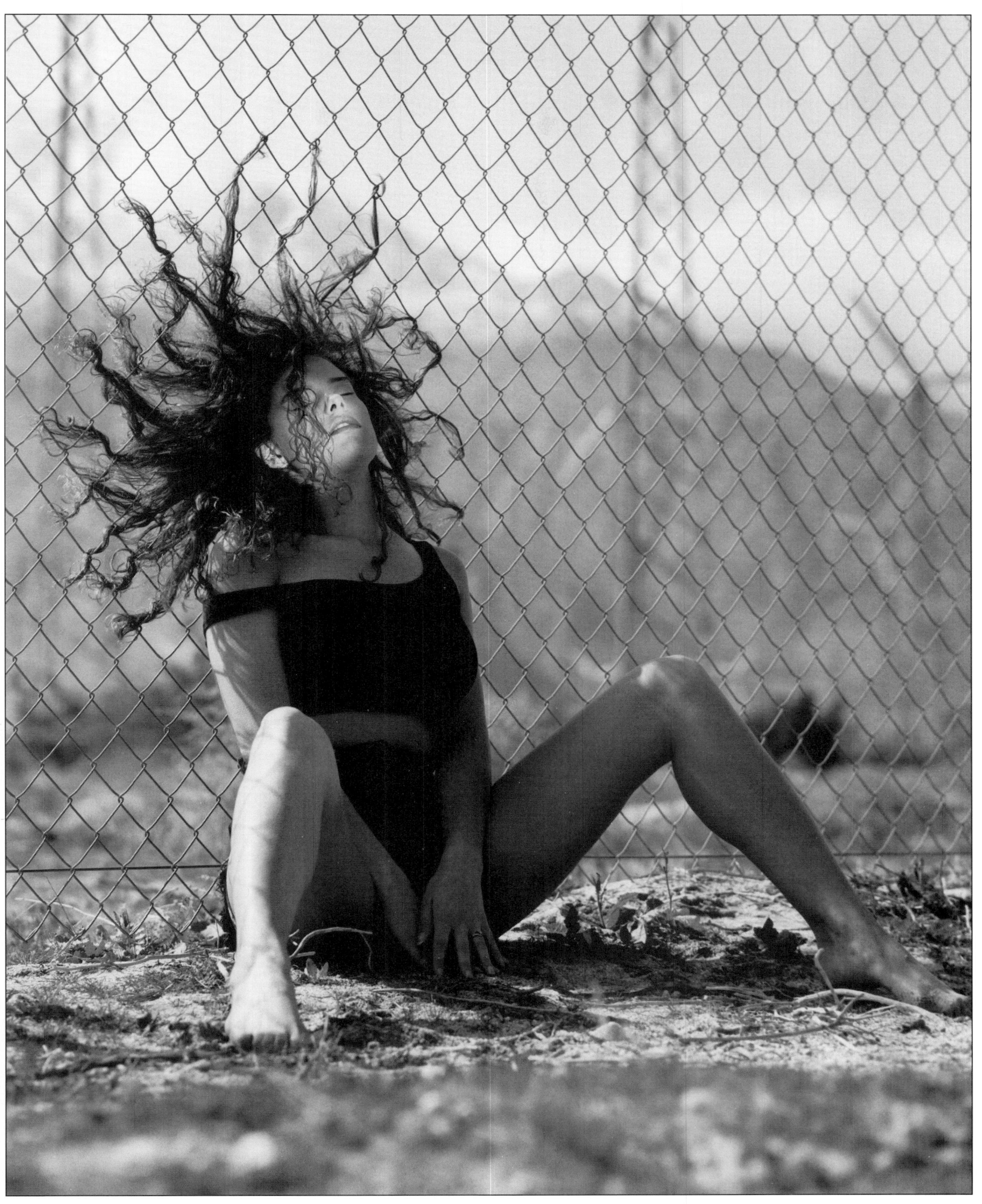

■ Assignment

This photograph was taken for a group of design-
ers. This dress is one that they made for a country
music star. I shot photos in order to put together a
promotional package for them.

■ Setting

We shot the photograph at a Stonehenge replica
in Washington state. The builder of the monument
recreated the landmark as though it were brand
new, rather than ancient and worn. It's a great
place to shoot.

■ Photography

I shot from the ground using a 28mm lens to get
this nice perspective.

■ Light

The photo shoot took place very early in the
morning when the sun was low in the sky. I used
only available light.

■ Posing

The wind kept coming up as we were shooting, so
I had the model pose to take advantage of it. The
wind blew back her dress and she lifted her arms
and tilted her head back to make it look like she's
really feeling the wind.

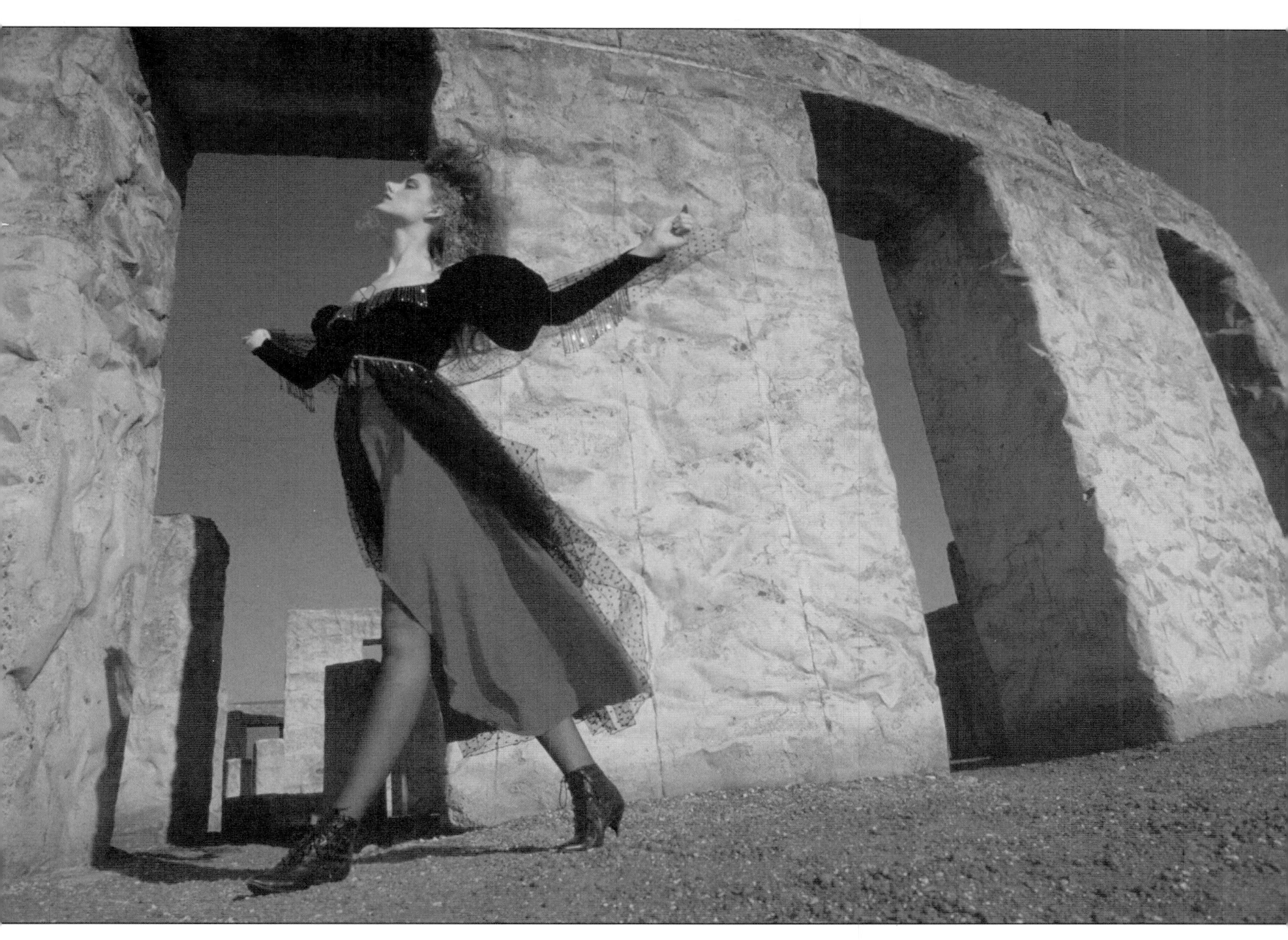

■ Assignment

This image was for the model's portfolio.

■ Background

The model was shot against a studio grey background. A red gel placed over a bare bulb was used to create the colored background. It was placed off to the left, behind the chair on which the model was seated. By dropping the light on the grey background (which picks up the color well), you can create backgrounds from red to pink. Colors other than reds also work well.

■ Lighting

The main light was an umbrella aimed straight at the model. Lighting a model's face straight on diminishes the appearance of her nose, here allowing the viewer to really focus on her beautiful eyes. A hair light was positioned above the model and set one stop hotter than the main. Although you cannot see the top of her head here, the light shows on her shoulder and helps separation.

■ Composition

A triangular composition was used, with the key points being the model's hair, shoulder and eye.

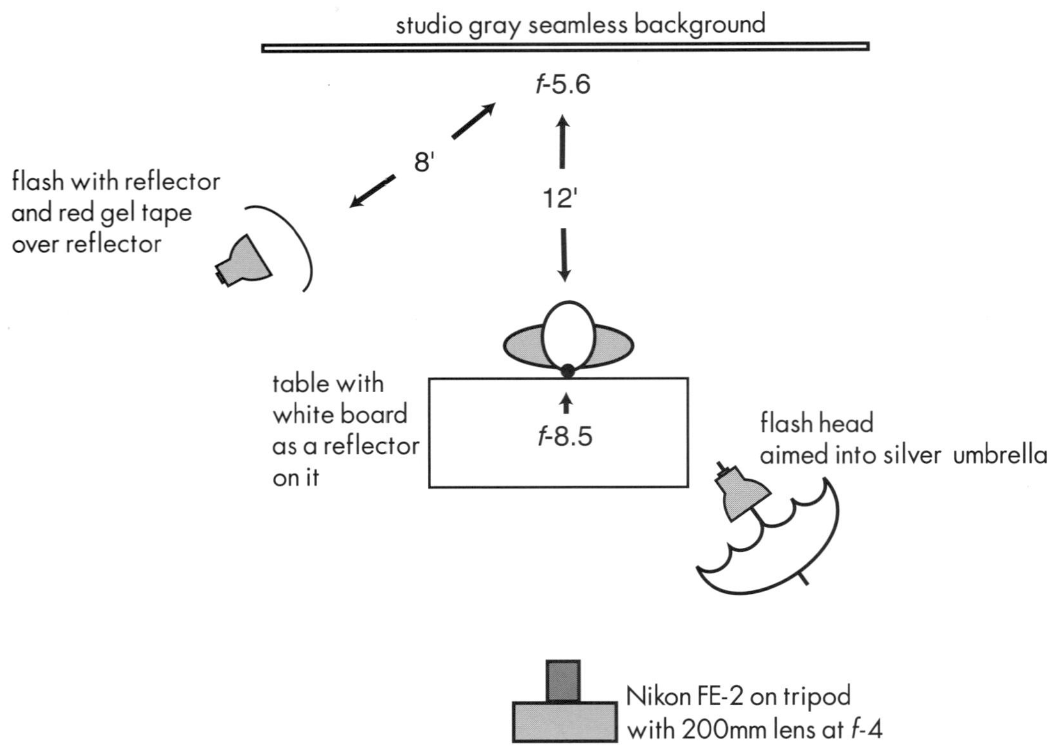

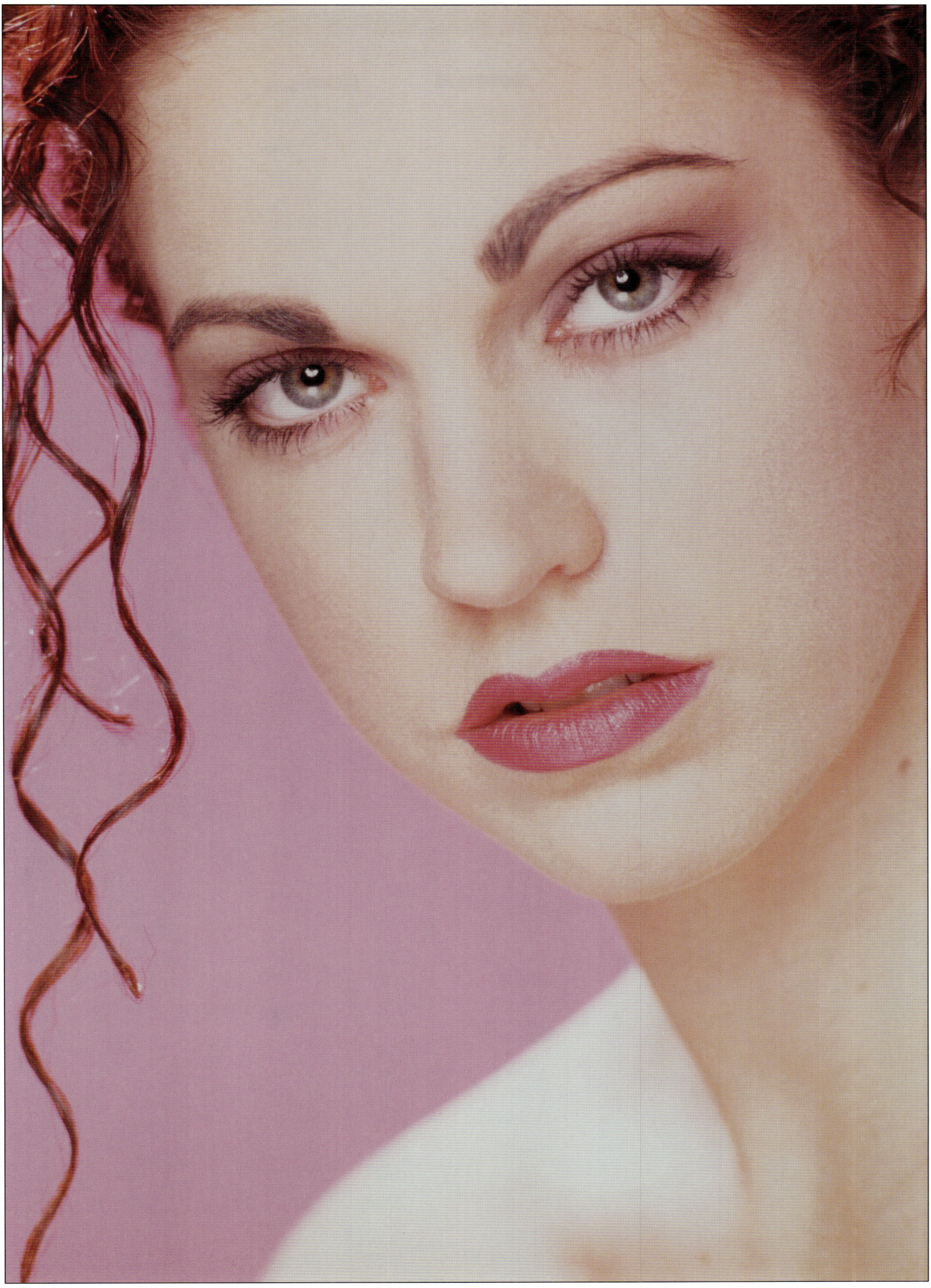

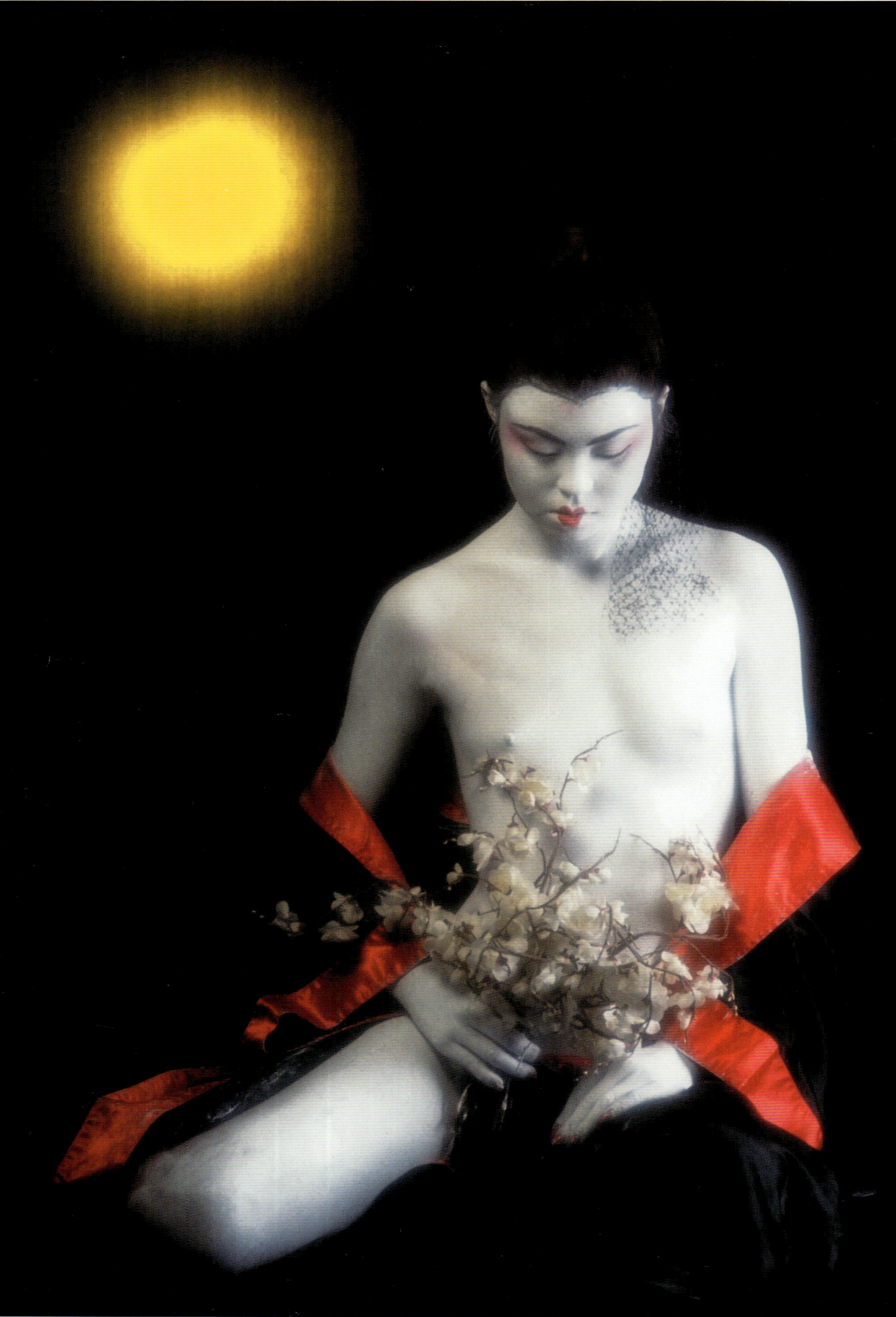

■ Assignment

This image was shot for a calendar.

■ Posing

The model was painted all over in white, creating a stark contrast between her body and the black scrim in the background. She was posed on a platform covered with black velvet.

■ Lighting

The special effect of the yellow moon glowing in the background was created entirely in the camera using a lighting technique I learned from the theater. The key to the effect is the backdrop. On the side near the model, I covered a 4'x8' frame with black scrim material. The opposite side was covered with tracing paper. One light with a bare bulb and a yellow gel was then directed from the back of the frame, through the tracing paper and scrim material. The paper spreads and softens the light, while the scrim material absorbs some of it. The result is a spot of bright color.

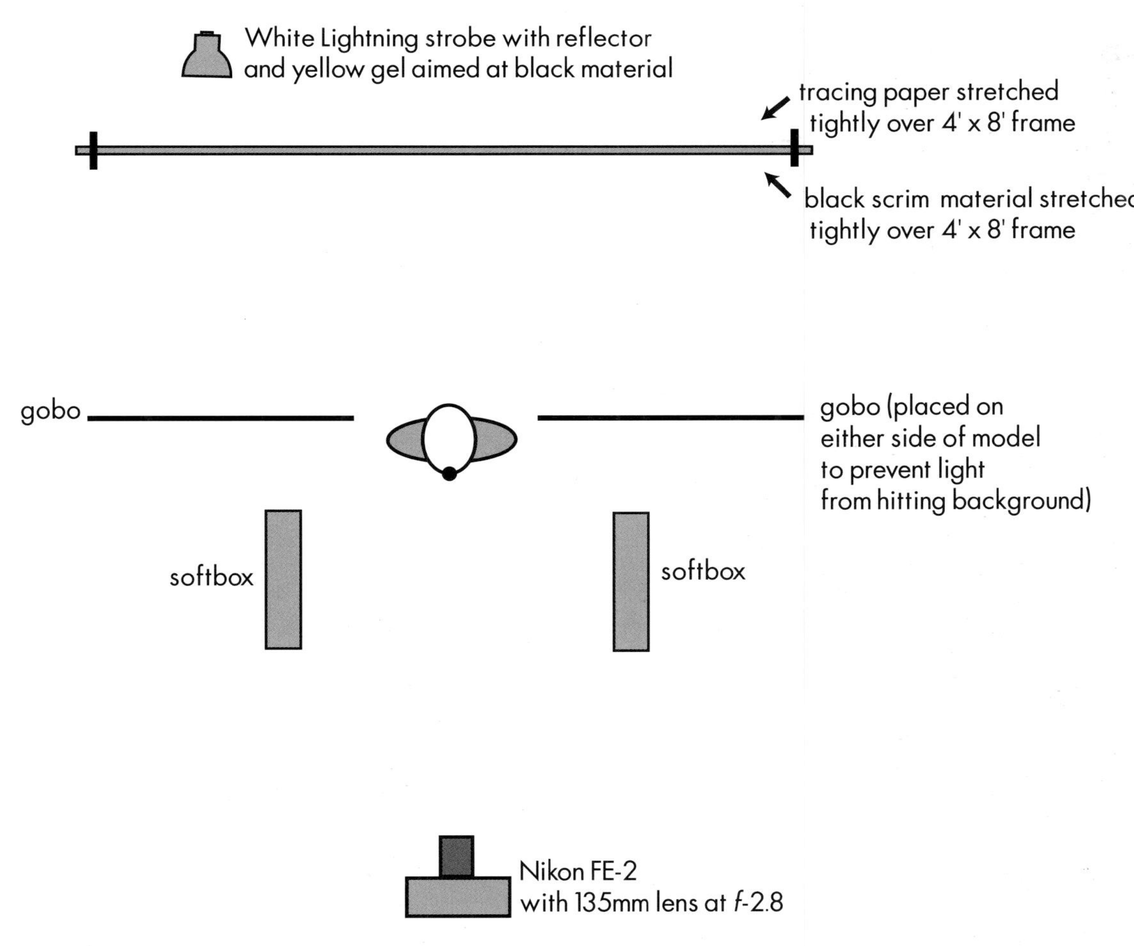

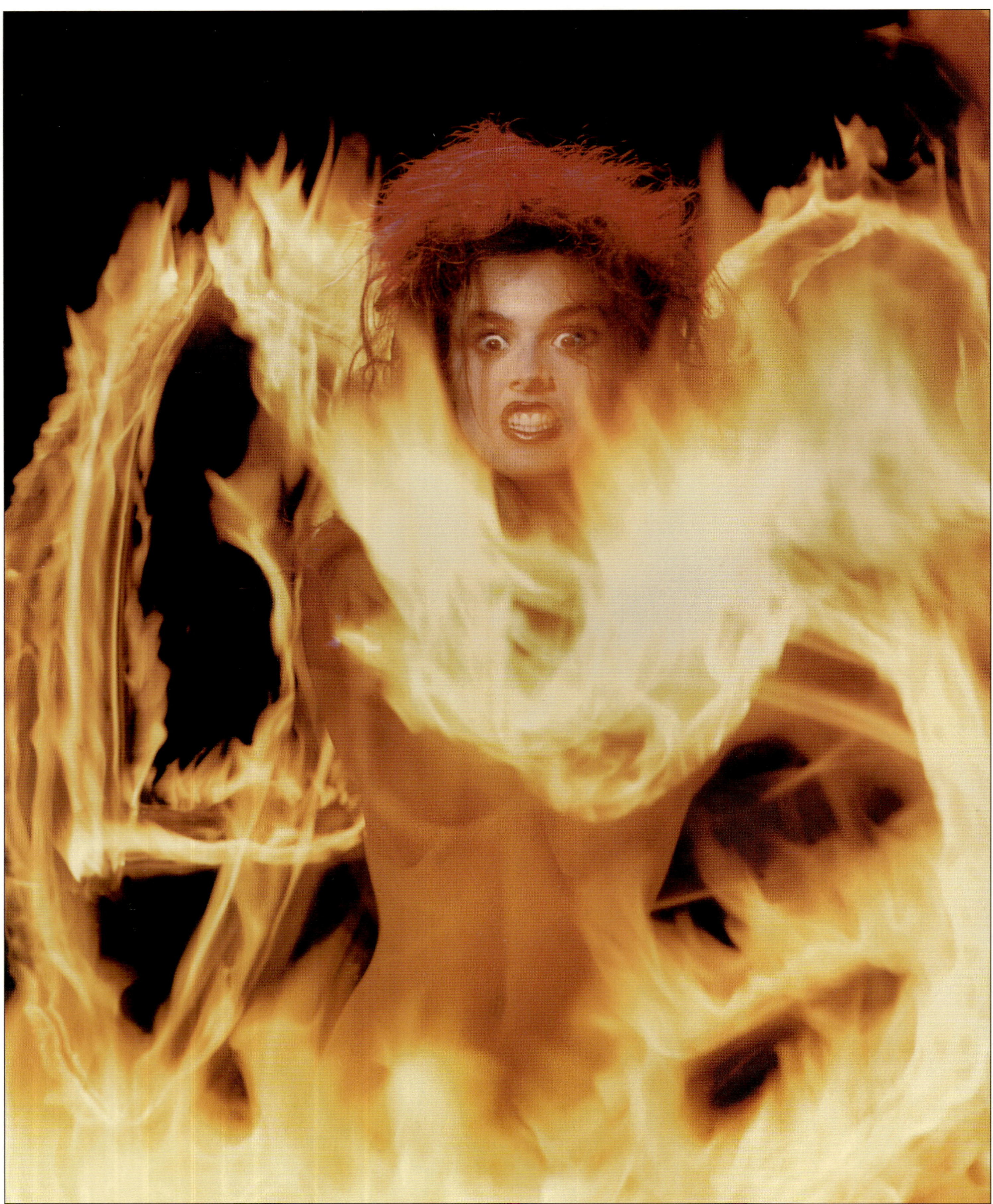

■ Photography

I shot this image with a Mamiya RB67 using Fuji 100 film rated at 64 . A 180mm lens was used for the photograph. While setting up the image I took a lot of Polaroids to ensure everything was set up properly.

■ Lighting

A flash was positioned over the model's head with a red filter to render her hair red. The light was hot — set at f-11. Two white lights were positioned to either side of the model. These were kept lower than her breasts and help separate the body from the other elements of the image. Each of these lights was fitted with an amber gel and set quite low (f-5.6). A white light was used at the camera. It was placed high and fitted with a grid spot reading f-8.

■ Fire

Shooting the image involved several steps. First, the room was totally darkened. I gave the model a countdown, at which point she opened her eyes and I triggered the flashes and left the camera open. While the shutter was open, I lit a piece of paper and spent about a minute walking around the model in front of the camera. Because the process is so involved, we only got about ten shots in three hours.

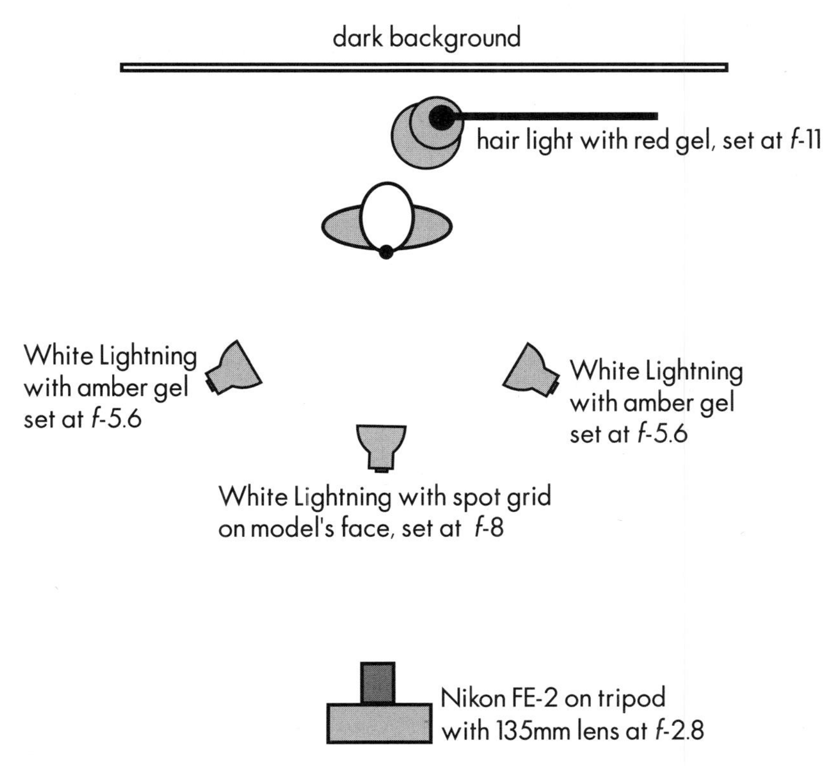

■ Assignment

This photograph was for the portfolio of a model who was going into the European markets. European posing standards are somewhat different from standards in the United States, so the image has a bit of a different flavor, reflected by the model's clothes and pose.

■ Setting

I had photographed the model on the ground, but felt that the background was too busy. Since the point of the photograph is to sell the model, it was important to make her strongly the focal part of the image. Posing the model on the truck helped to separate her from the background, as does her elevation and distance from the camera.

■ Posing

The pose shows off her legs.

■ Lighting

The image uses only natural light. It was shot on a beautiful grey day in Seattle.

■ Photography

The image was shot with a Nikon F3 camera with a 300mm lens and PlusX film.

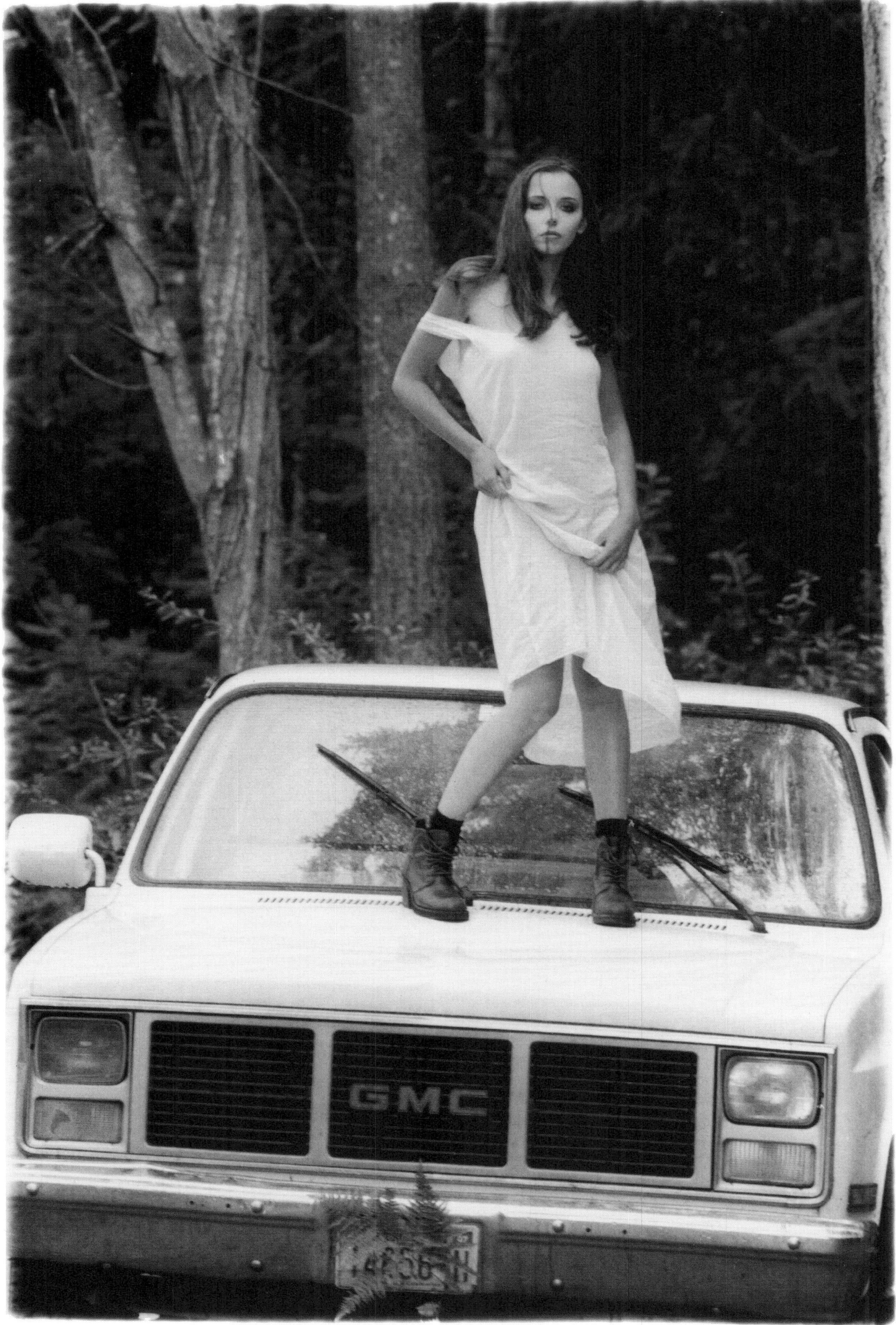

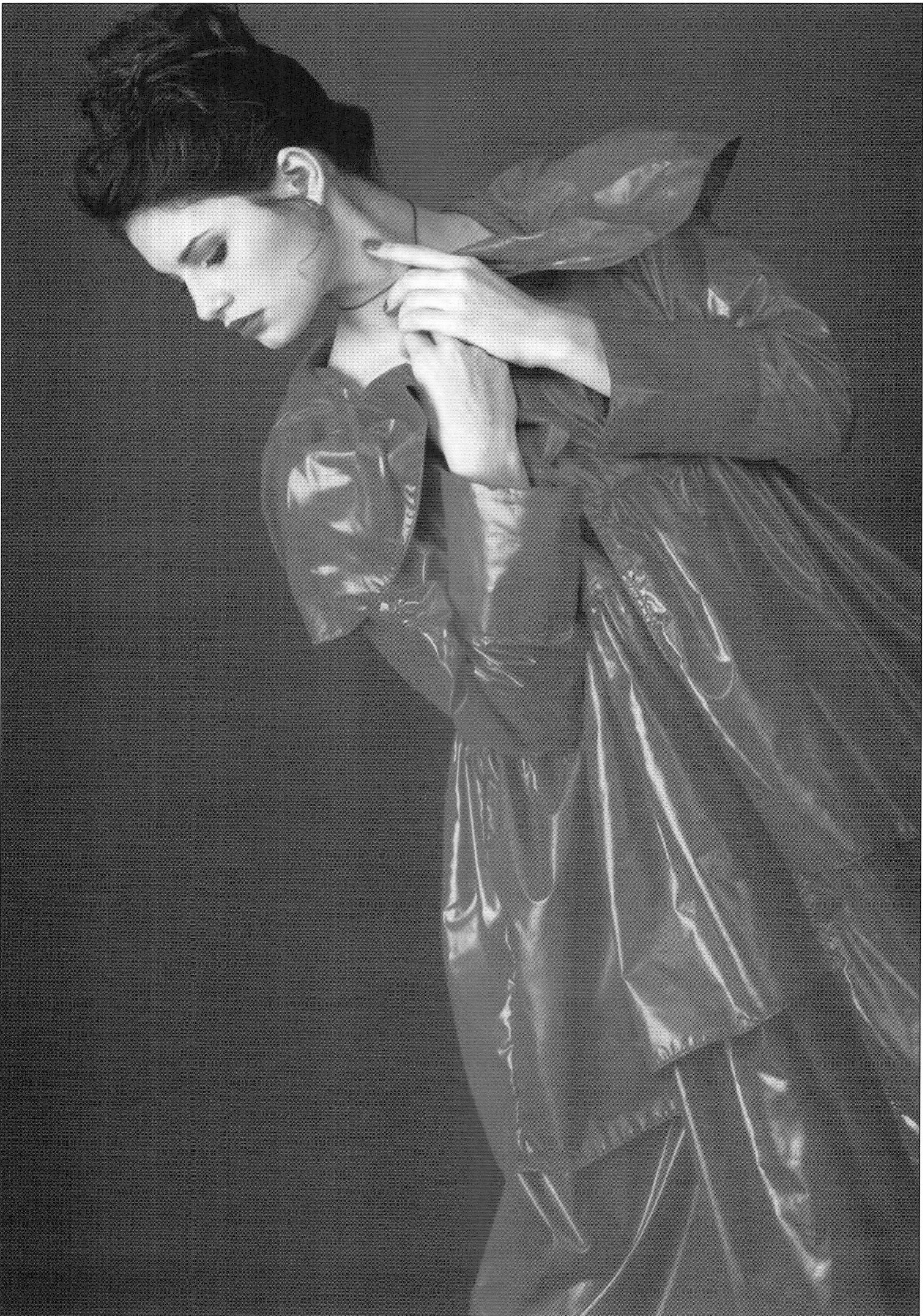

■ Assignment

This photograph was taken for the Seattle designer who produced this coat.

■ Lighting

A narrow rectangular soft box was placed to the left of the model. The background was set to one stop darker than the model in order to create separation between it and the model. A hair light was placed above the model on a boom. The light from this falls on her hair and shoulders.

■ Clothing

The coat didn't hang quite right on this model, so we had to have a person lay on the floor at the feet of the model and hold the hem of the coat so it hung properly. This is quite common. When shooting a model in baggy jeans, the front of the pants often have to be held from the bottom to make them look right. Using an assistant to hold clothing can also allow you to create a sense of movement without having to use a fan.

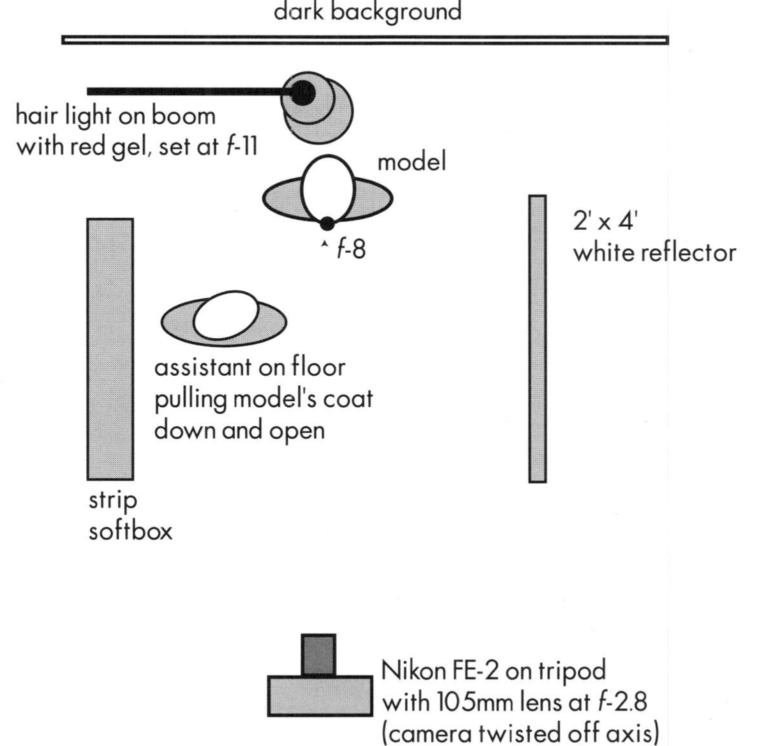

■ Assignment

The client for whom this photograph was taken re-designs and embellishes men's clothes for women. She was having a problem attracting the business she wanted among young women. Thus, we chose a young model with a belly ring and braided her hair. The image is fun and fresh and young.

■ Lighting

A soft box was placed to the right of the model. This side lighting results in a nice representa-tion of the texture of the clothing. A small white light was used above the model. This throws light onto the model's shoulder and helps to separate her from the dark background (especially visible on her left shoulder). The light was about 1 stop lighter than the main, and was positioned to hit the back of the model's neck.

■ Background

The background used was a dark blue paper which was not lit.

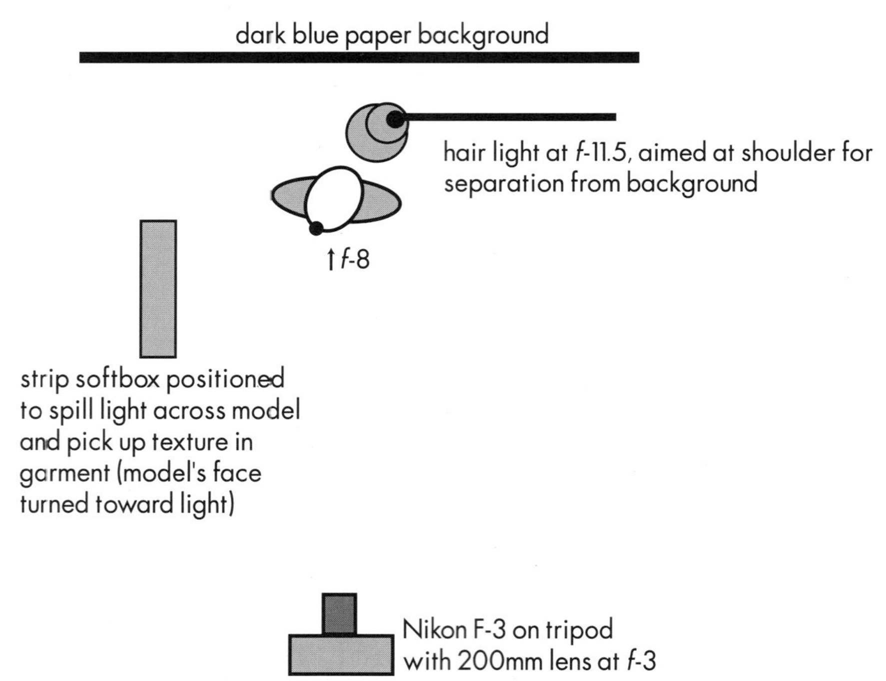

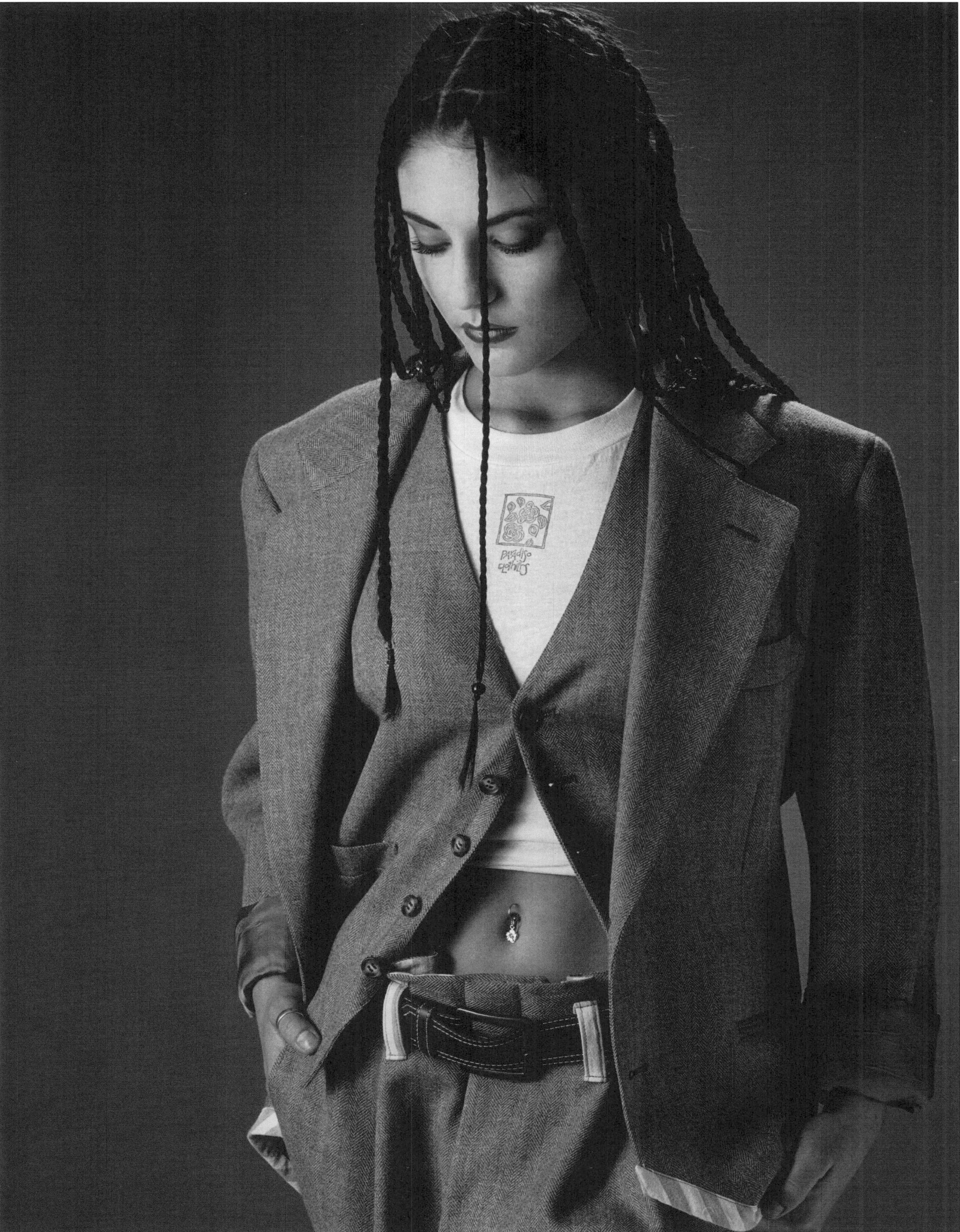
paradiso

■ Assignment

This photograph was used by an actress in her portfolio.

■ Posing

Basically, she was just playing around! I took the shot while she was leaning up against a window.

■ Location

The actress and I were walking around in a hotel.

■ Lighting

I used a Sun Pack 522 camera flash aimed straight on. I had someone hold the flash higher than the camera.

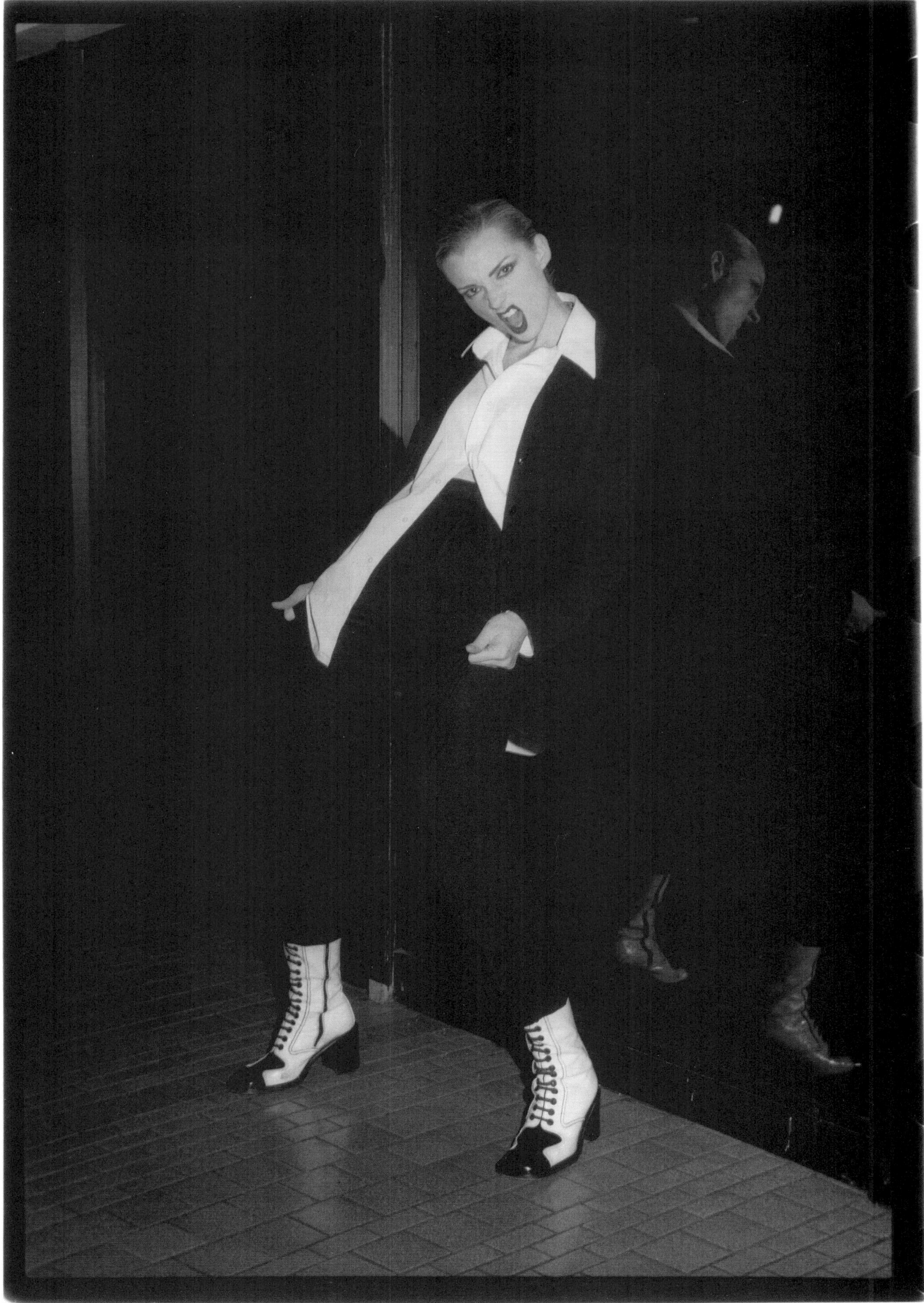

■ Background

The model was posed in front of white seamless paper.

■ Lighting

White paper reflects a great deal more light than human skin. Since I wanted a silhouette, I exposed the shot for the paper and did not light the subject at all. After metering, you will want to spot down one stop or you will get too much light reflected off the background, reducing the overall contrast on your subject. You will also want to bracket the image well.

■ Printing

Select the best exposure and print the image such that the model's figure goes completely black.

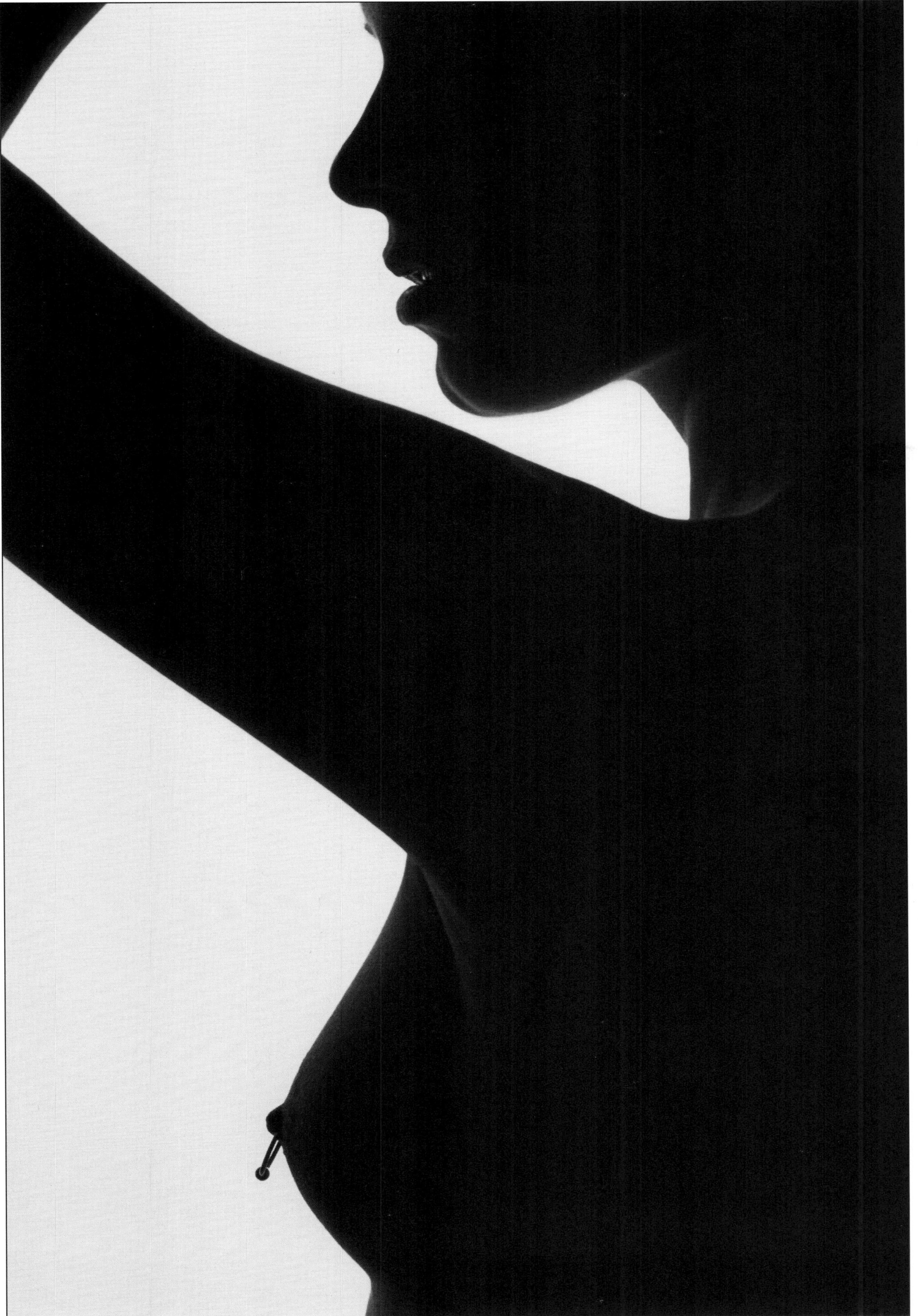

■ Assignment

The shoot was for the model's portfolio, but I also later used the image on my business cards. The image has gotten me a lot of business, including an account with Filc, who saw my business card with this image pinned to an advertising agency wall (where a former model of mine had put it!).

■ Setting

The model was posed in the studio in front of an old barn wall. Light shines on him through an old window frame.

■ Lighting

In order to get the nice shadows you see here, you have to use a very hard light. A soft box just won't produce these. To produce the light for this image I used a flash tube, but in a special way. Since a flash tube is almost a full circle, pointing it straight on at the subject won't produce a hard edged shadow. This is because of its circular shape, which acts almost like two lights hitting from both sides. To compensate for this, I turn the light on its edge, and aim the *side* of the bare bulb at the model. I then screened the rest of the light from the camera and the subject. You lose about a stop of light with this technique, but get great hard shadows.

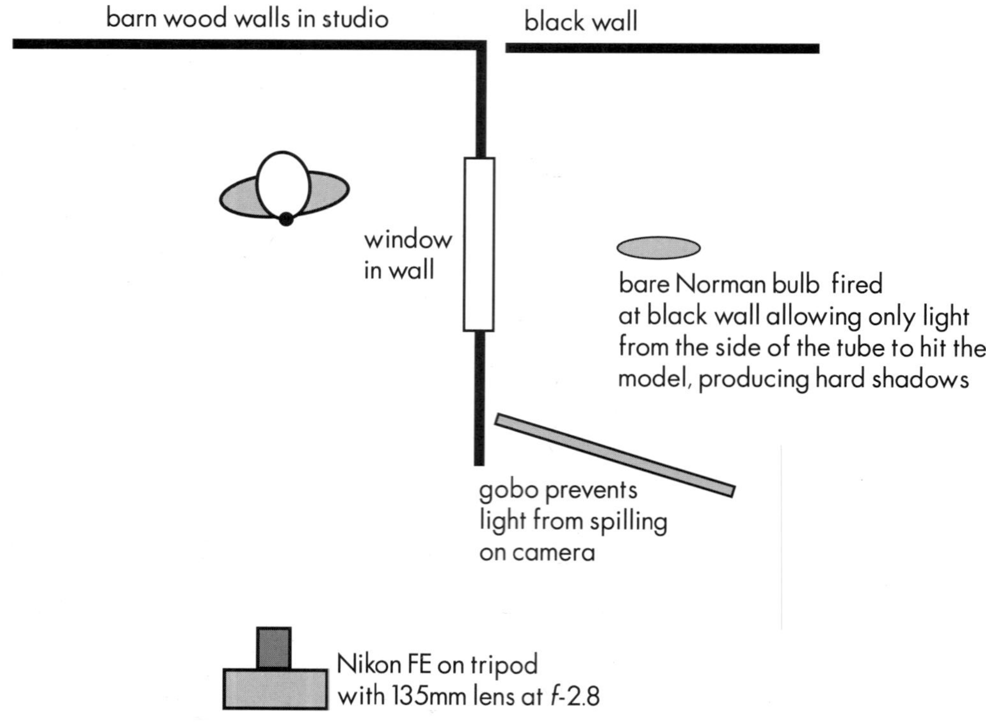

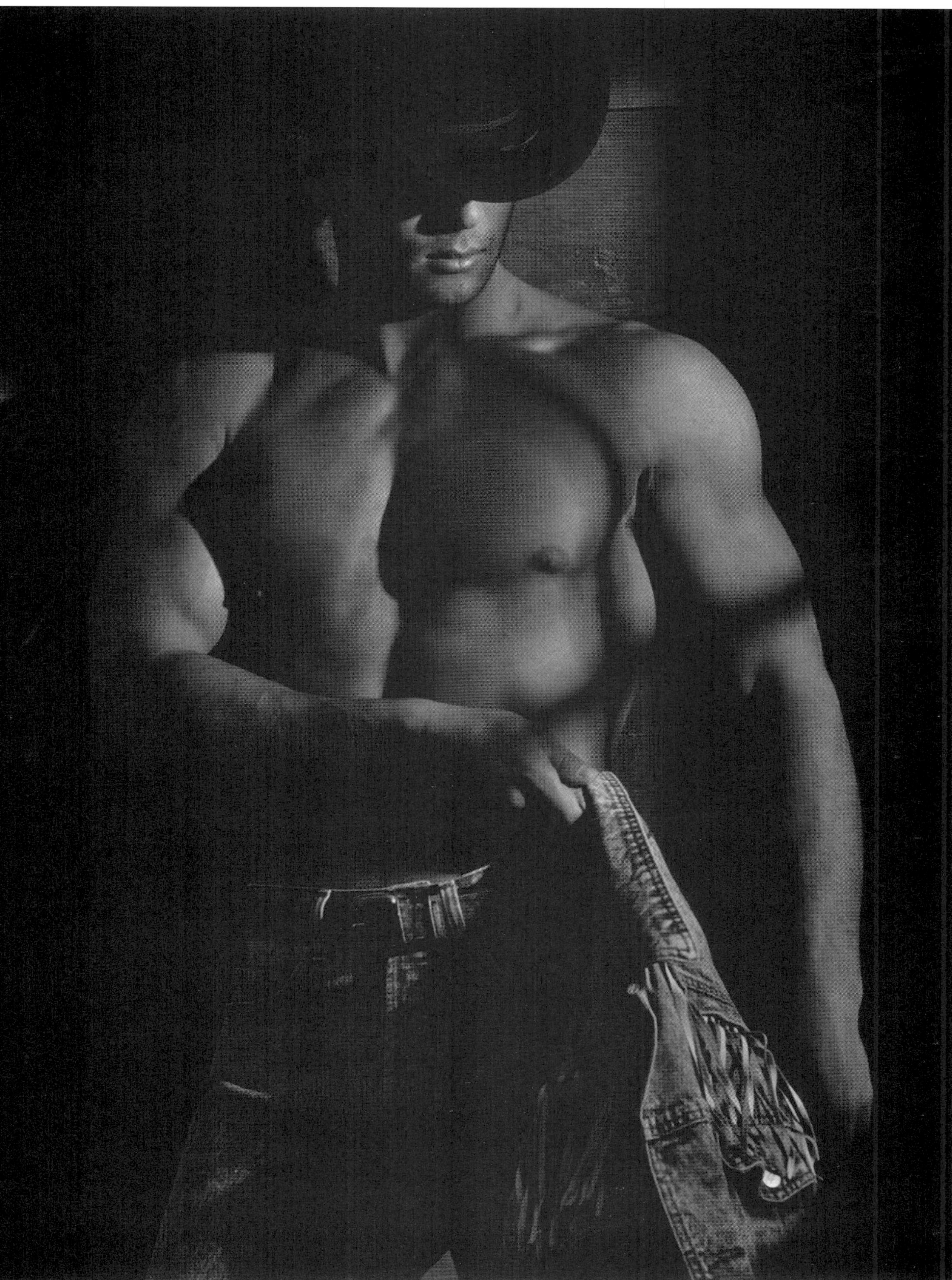

■ Assignment

This image was taken for the model's portfolio.

■ Lighting

A small, square, 12" soft box was positioned straight on to get nice dark shadows with a bit of a hard edge.

■ Background

The background used was a dark grey seamless paper.

■ Printing

I printed the final image using a sepia bleach process. I first printed the image about two stops darker than I wanted the final print. I burned in the background even more, so that when bleaching, the model would come out more quickly. I then used a sepia bleach on the print and fixed the final image.

■ Border

The printed border on the image, which also shows the sprocket holes, forces the eye back into the photograph. This is important because the background in the image is so even.

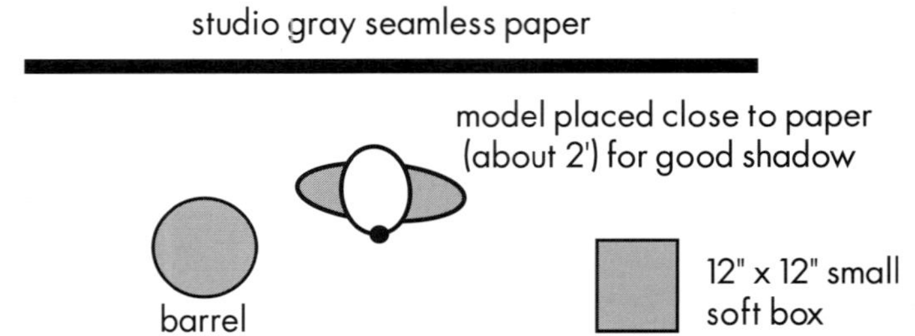

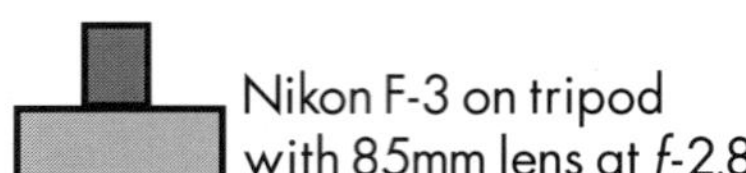

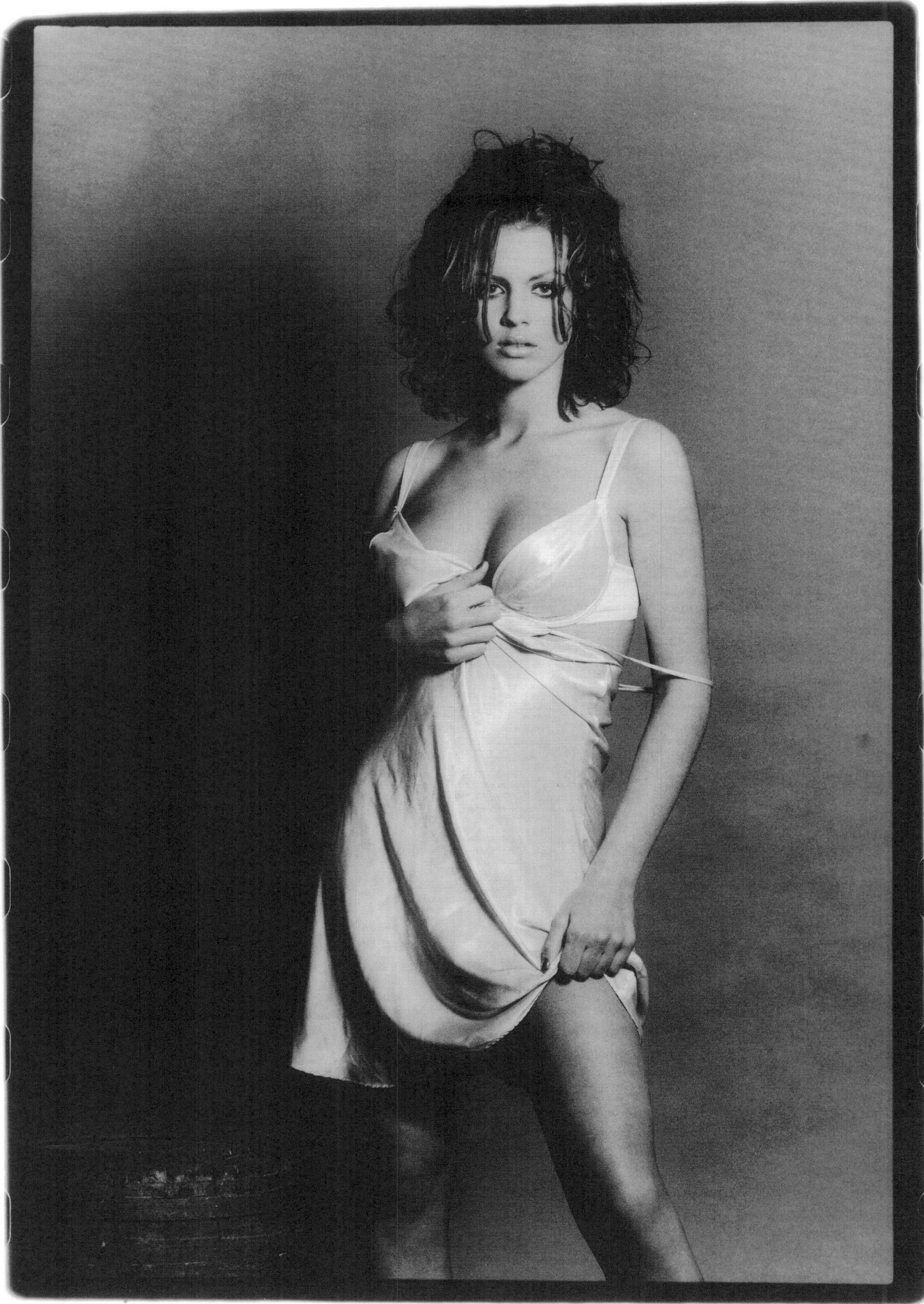

■ Inspiration

The idea for this photograph came from some colored string I found at a craft shop. I thought it would look interesting in a photo.

■ Lighting

An umbrella was placed off to the right of the model.

■ Photography

The image was shot using Elite 100 film. I overexposed the shot one full stop in order to produce a very clean skin tone.

■ Background

The model was posed in front of white seamless paper.

■ Portfolio

A model's portfolio should not be shot by only one photographer. A good book must include a variety of images with different hair styles, different make up, different clothes and different moods. This is not something you can do in one shoot, with one photographer. Therefore, it's helpful if you can recommend other good photographers in your area, especially to models who are putting together their first book. I try to give the models five or six good images and get them to a point where they are comfortable working with other photographers and being in front of the camera.

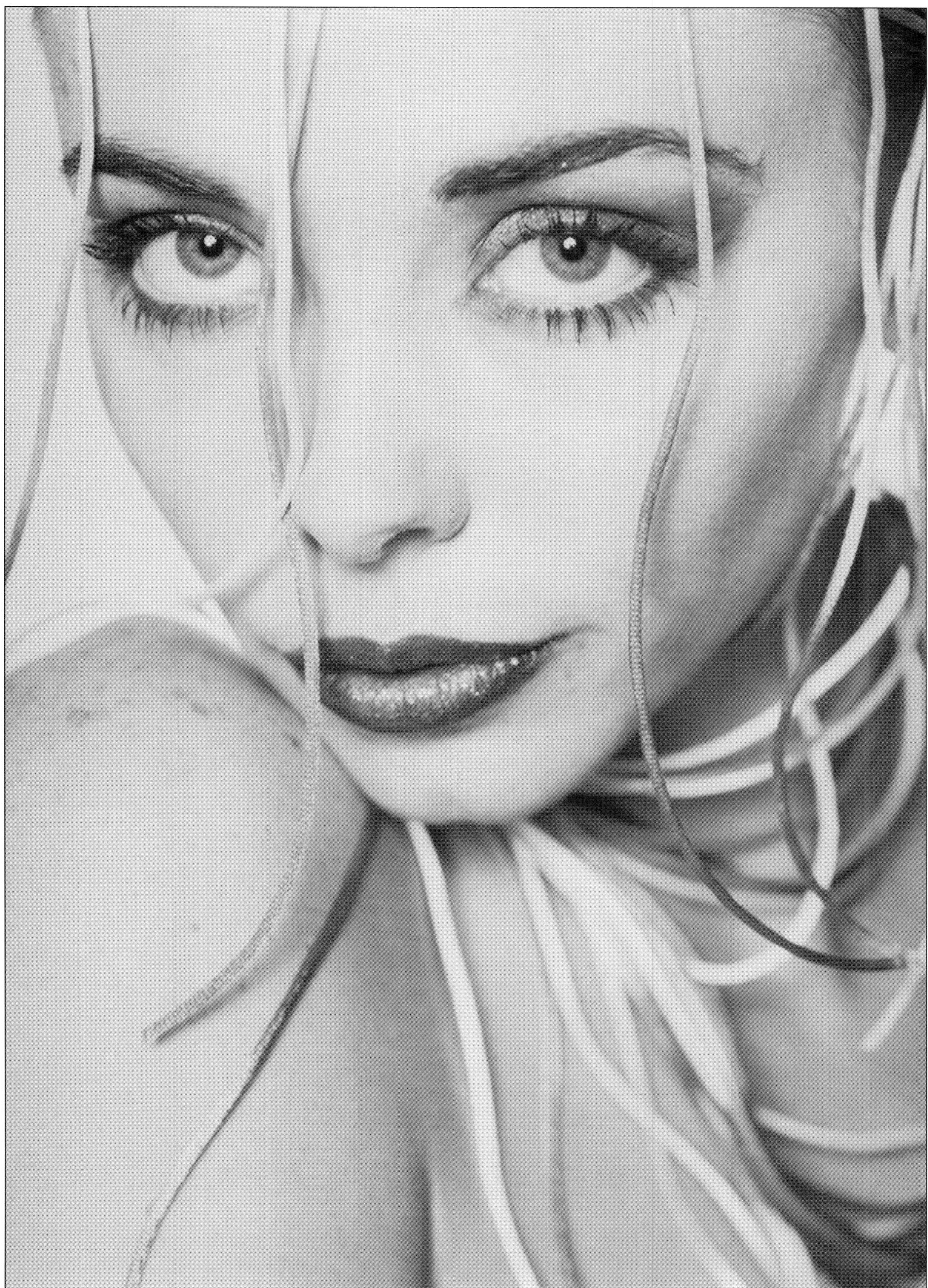

■ Concept

My idea here was to show a sculpture in progress; something not quite completed. That's why you see the sculptor's tool still stuck in his work on the left side of the image. I've done several other clay images like this (a whole gallery show, in fact). People often assume that the shots are actually of sculpture, and not of living models.

■ Lighting

Two soft boxes illuminate the clay-covered model from above.

■ The Shoot

To do the shot, I brought 200lbs of clay into the studio. It took five people about four hours to cover the model's body in clay (the model actually fell asleep while we were doing it). The model's hair was covered in plastic, so the clay hair you see is entirely sculpted. The clay had to be kept constantly wet by use of a spritzer bottle.

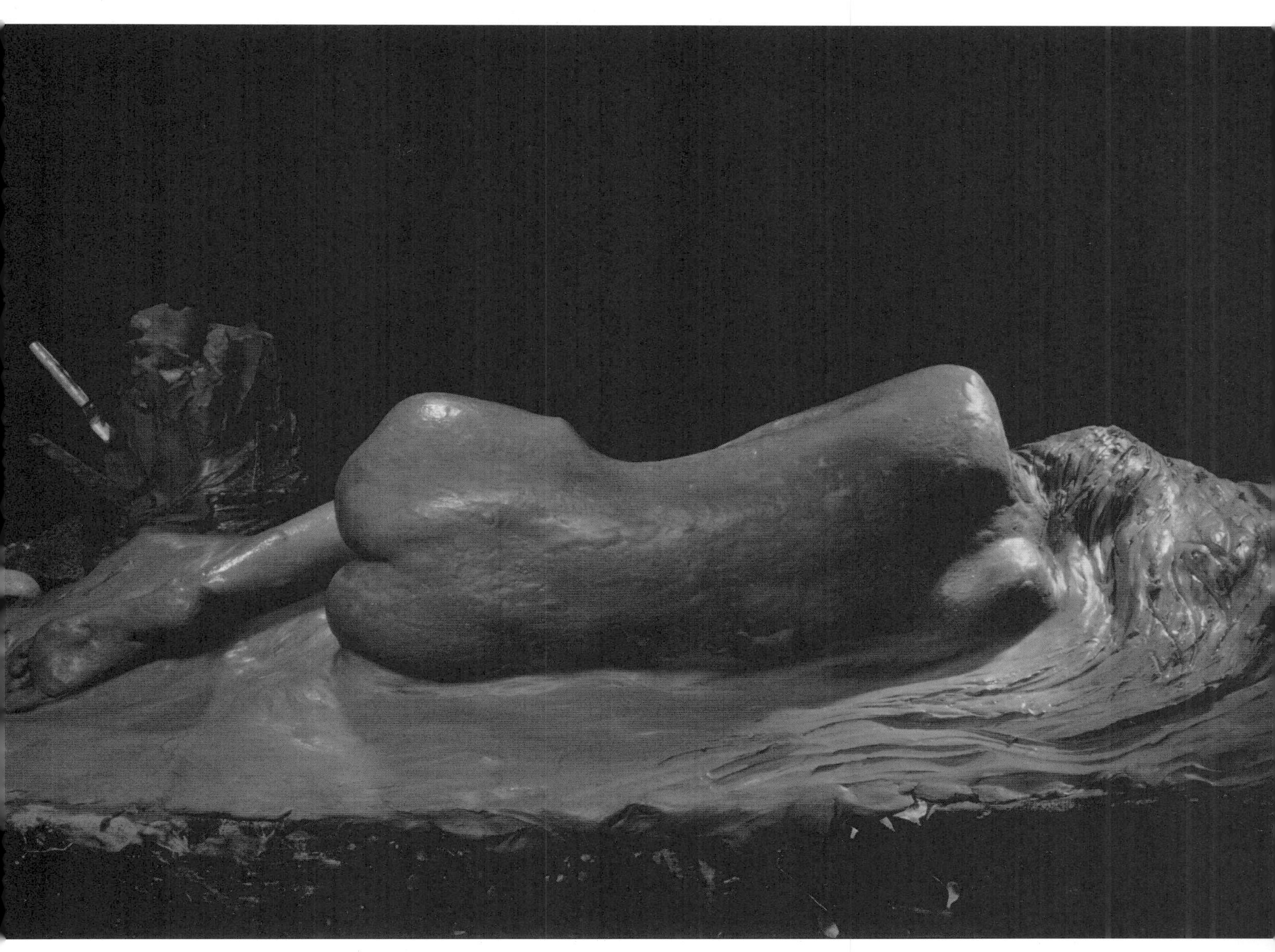

■ Assignment

This image was shot of and for an artist who wanted figure studies from which to paint.

■ Lighting

The light for this photograph was provided by one soft box positioned low to the camera.

■ Background

The model was posed on a dark grey canvas.

■ Posing

The pose downplays the model's face, but draws attention to her knees, which are turned toward the camera, and her arms, which cradle her body.

■ Printing

The pose was further emphasized in printing by allowing the model's face to go quite dark.

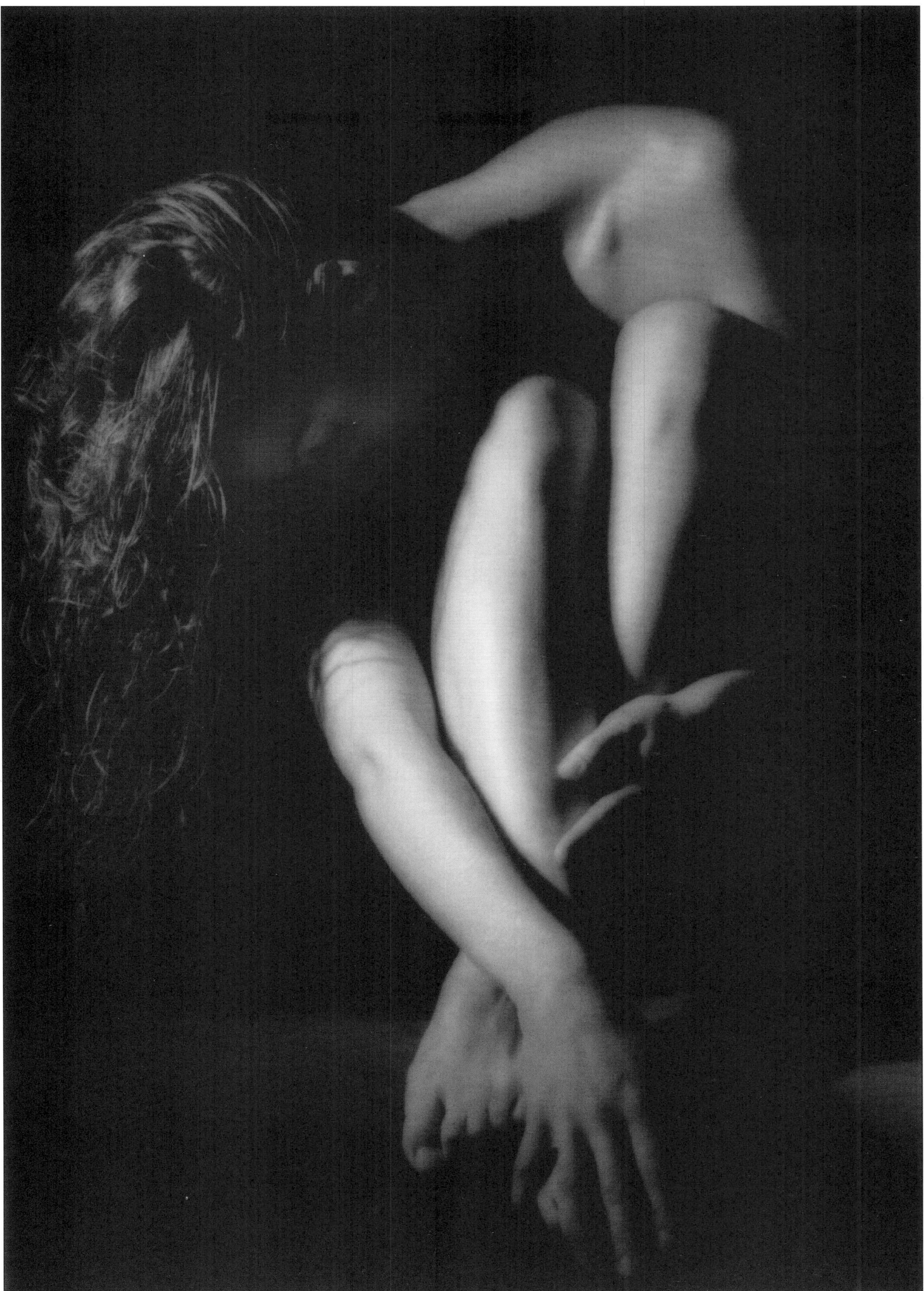

■ Lighting

The model was lit using a soft box to her right, positioned low to the camera.

■ Printing

To achieve the interesting texture, the image was printed through a screen.

■ Posing

It is important to be very descriptive with posing. Being in front of the camera can make people nervous, but being clear with your instructions and making the session professional can really help. A trick to try is to have another person stand in for the model and allow the model to look through the camera so she can see what you are seeing and understand the posing. Finally, you may even try having the model pose while there is no film in the camera, if that helps to relieve anxiety about the shoot. Once underway shooting, don't have the model change poses dramatically for every shot. Rather, ask her to change one small element per shot — perhaps the tilt of her head, the position of her hand, the angle of her hips, etc..

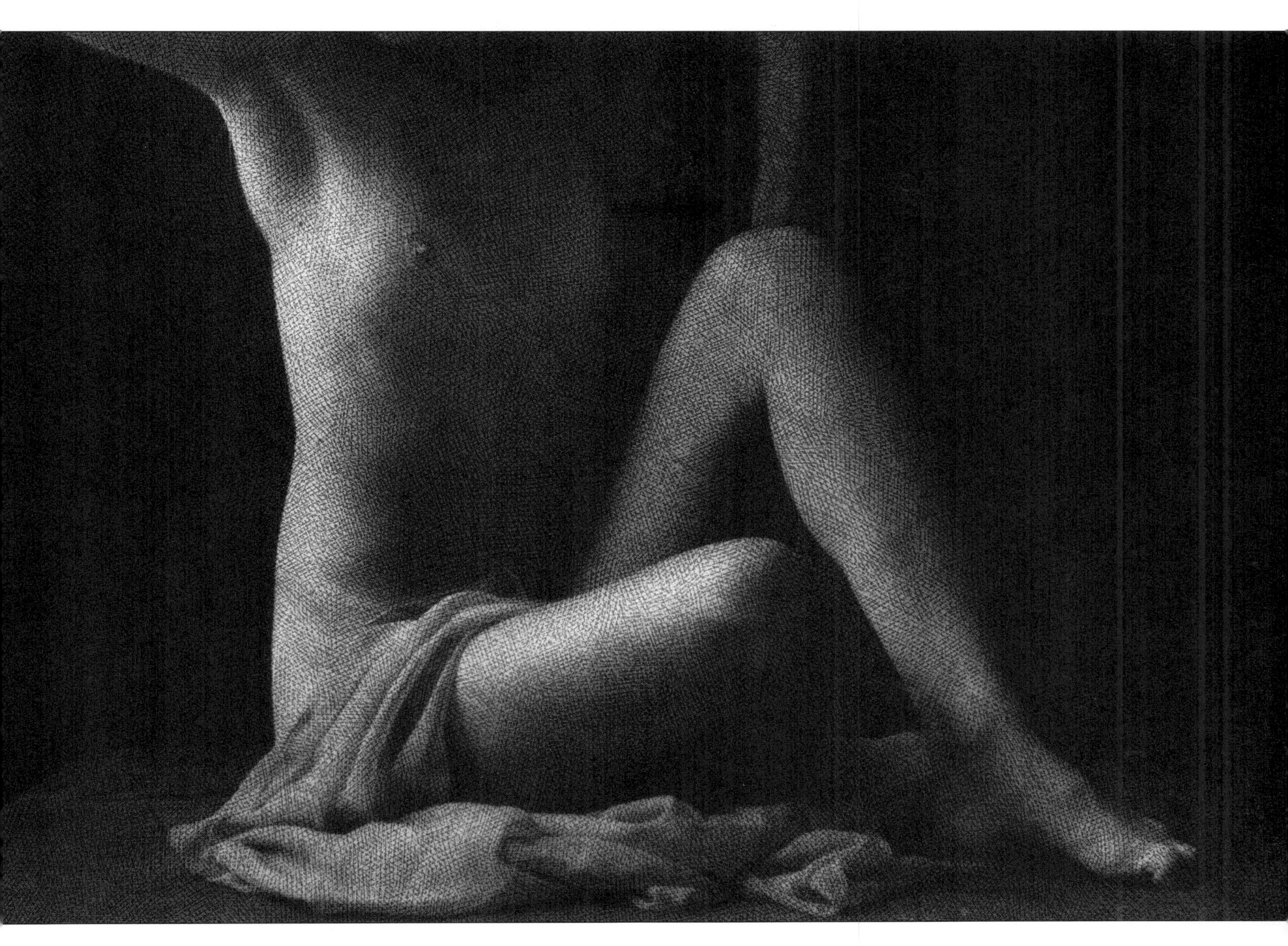

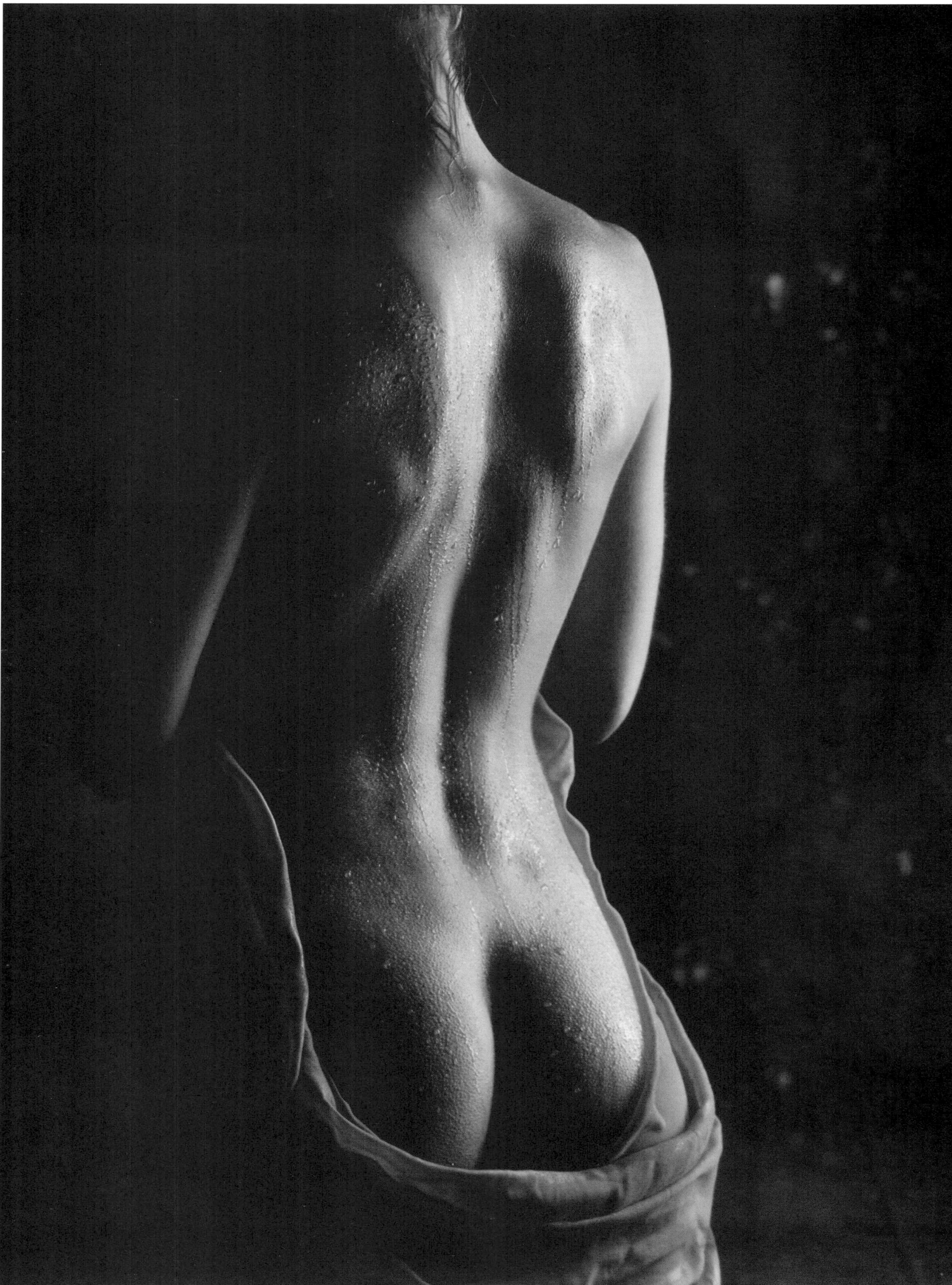

■ Lighting

The model was illuminated with a softbox to her right.

■ Posing

For this image, the model was covered with baby oil, then spritzed with water. The baby oil is used in order to make the water bead well on her skin.

The fabric used was also wet down. This makes it much easier to arrange correctly, and helps it conform more closely to the curves of the model's body.

■ Printing

As with most of my fine art images, I printed this about a stop darker than I would have for a normal image to be used in a portfolio.

■ Posing

The model was posed sitting on an 18 inch tall raised platform. This allowed me to shoot at her straight on. I draped the cloth over her head and had her arch her back a little.

■ Lighting

A soft box was placed to the left of the model. This lighting from the side ensures that you will get good texture on the cloth.

■ Background

The background is dark gray canvas.

■ Cloth

I tried an image like this with white cloth, but found that it created too high a contrast with the model's skin. In order to get the detail I wanted, I had to print the image much too dark. To compensate, for this and future images I switched to a purple cloth which photographs as a middle grey.

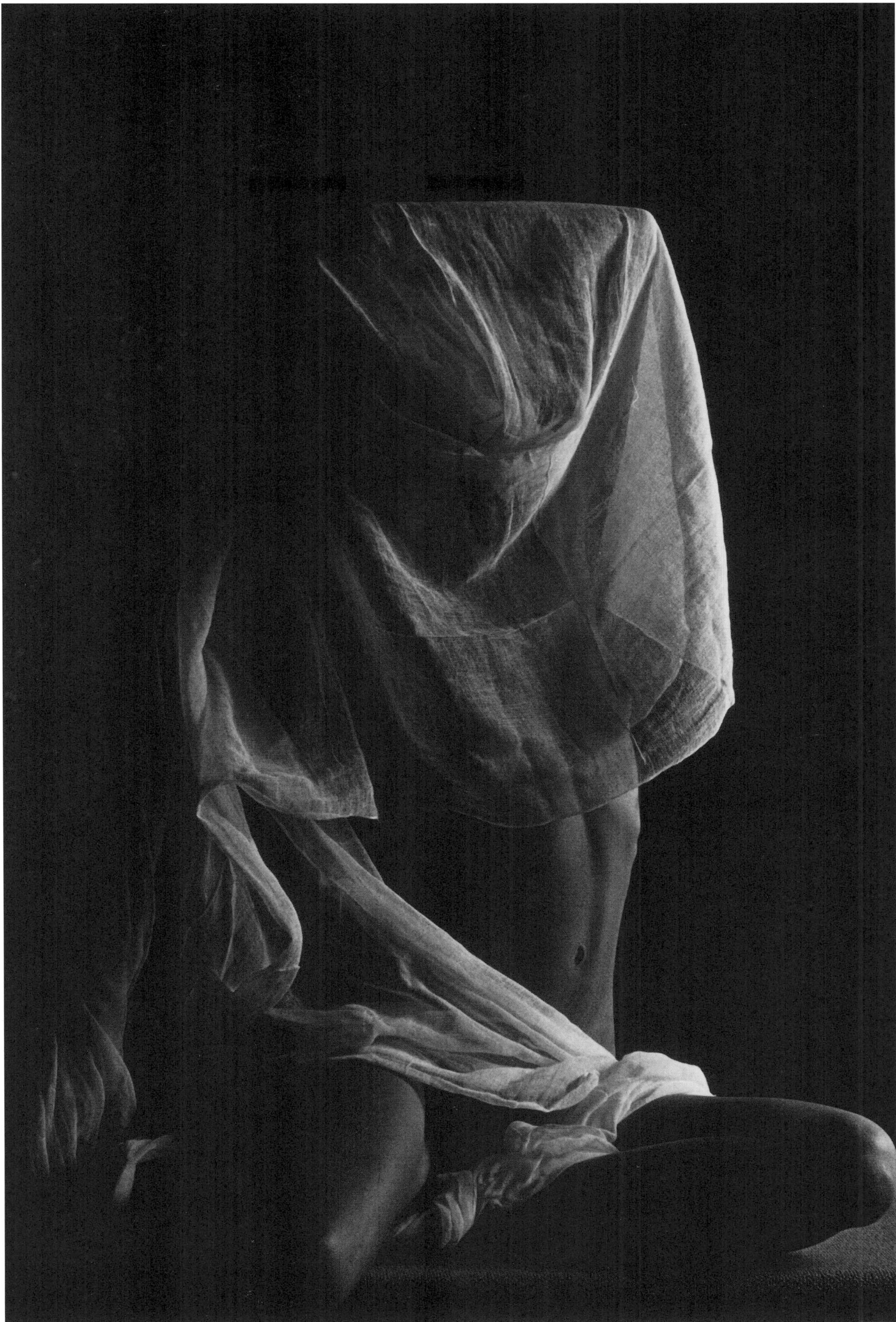

■ Posing

I had the model stand on a concrete pedestal I have in my studio.

■ Lighting

One soft box lights the model from her left.

■ Special Effect

The effect of the model's body being "broken off" at the upper torso was created using a torn piece of paper to crop off the upper body. To achieve the pixelated effect, I used a special screen while printing the image.

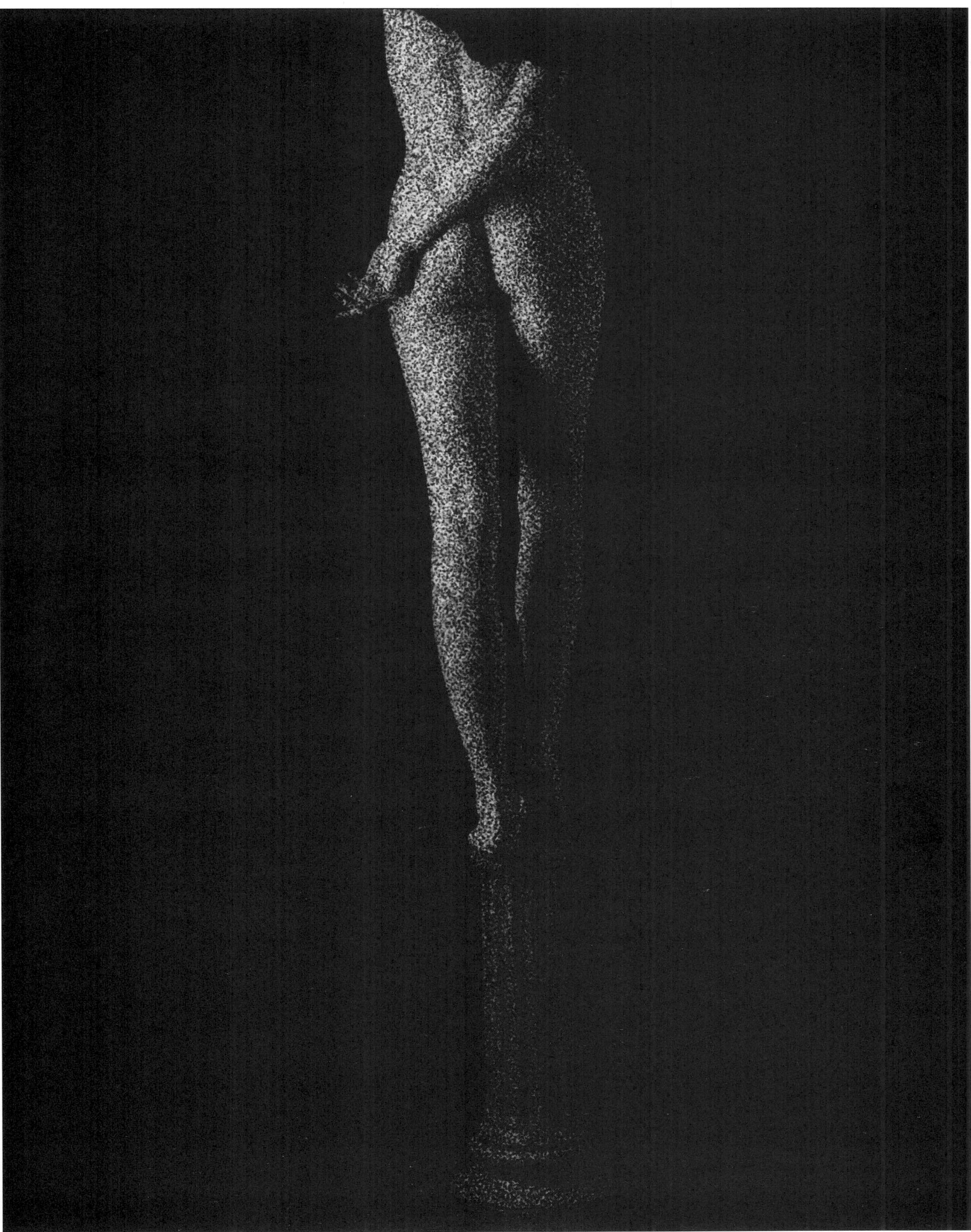

Credits

pg. 7, 51: model, Marisa Clayton; client, Steven Christian Hair Salon.
pg. 9: model, Francesca Helina; agency, Gyre and Gimble, Seattle, WA.
pg. 11, pg. 53: model, Torie Howard; agency, Premier Models, Salt Lake City, UT.
pg. 13: model, Mary Carter.
pg. 14: model, Rachel Nielsen; agency, Premier Models, Salt Lake City, UT.
pg. 17: model, Valerie Bauman; agency, Gyre and Gimble, Seattle, WA.
pg. 19: models, Jeani Link and Shannon Talbot; client, T-N-T Guns, Phoenix, AZ.
pg. 20: model, Scott Laughlin.
pg. 22, pg 34-35: model, Jennifer Arnold; agency, Gyre and Gimble, Seattle, WA.
      (pg. 34-35: mother, Suzanne Arnold; assistants, Jennie Burkie, Wade Wolcott)
pg. 25: model, Holly Braithwaite; agency, Gyre and Gimble, Seattle, WA.
pg. 27: model, Elspeth Horn; agency, Gyre and Gimble, Seattle, WA.
pg. 29: model, Kimberly Davies; agency, Premier Models, Salt Lake City, UT.
pg. 30: model, Annie Swenson; agency, Premier Models, Salt Lake City, UT.
pg. 33, pg. 49: model, Lindsay Kozlowski; agency, Pizzazz, Saskatoon, SK, Canada.
pg. 38: model, Danielle VanDobben.
pg. 40: model, Geneva Somers.
pg. 42, pg. 43: model, Julie Brown (pg. 43: client, Steven Christian Hair Salon)
pg. 45: model, Eryn Hanson; agency, Andersen Models International; client, Uland Arts Inc.
pg. 47: model, Debra Jones; client, Brent David Designs, New Orleans, LA.
pg. 50: model, Jami Crain; client, SP&M Company Hair Designs, Willie Moralis.
pg. 54: model, Tish Tinker
pg. 56: model, Scarlett Johnson; client, T-N-T Guns.
pg. 59, pg. 71: model, Lisa Whitney; agency, Gyre and Gimble, Seattle, WA.
pg. 61: model, Ambra McNamee.
pg. 63: model, Adrienne McBride; agency, Premier Models, Salt Lake City, UT.
pg. 67: model, Stephanie Rector; agency, Arizona Bikini Team.
pg. 68: model, Barbara Nelson.
pg. 74: model, Carrie Cole.
pg. 77: models, Lisa Martin and Danielle Salada-Hooper; clients, Ellen Lam Designs, Steven Christian Hair Design
pg. 79: model, Jennifer Griffith.
pg. 81: model, Shelia Cagle; client, Phillip Michael Salon.
pg. 83: model, Kelly Lovall; client, Xsintrics Clothing; hair design by Willie Moralis, PM & Company.
pg. 85: model, Emily Lathen.
pg. 88: model, Elizabeth Vargas; agency, Kim Brooke Group.
pg. 29: model, Kimberly Davies; agency, Premier Models, Salt Lake City, UT.
pg. 91: pg 105: model, Janeen Mitzen; agency, Gyre and Gimble, Seattle, WA.
pg. 94: model, Wendy Basarab; client, Ellen Lam Fashions.
pg. 95: model, Shannon Brown; agency, Bobbie Brown Agency, Los Angeles, CA.
pg. 99: model, Heidi Hedlund.
pg. 101: model, Glen Bayer.
pg. 103: model, Julie Brown.
pg. 107: model, Lynda Jean.

Other Books from Amherst Media, Inc.

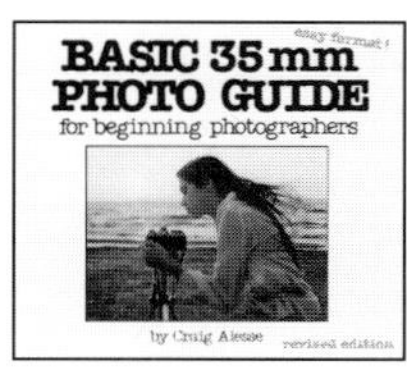

Basic 35mm Photo Guide

Craig Alesse

Great for beginning photographers! Designed to teach 35mm basics step-by-step — completely illustrated. Includes: 35mm automatic and semi-automatic cameras, camera handling, *f*-stops, shutter speeds, and more! $12.95 list, 9x8, 112p, 178 photos, order no. 1051.

Build Your Own Home Darkroom

Lista Duren & Will McDonald

This classic book shows how to build a high quality, inexpensive darkroom in your basement, spare room, or almost anywhere. Information on: darkroom design, woodworking, tools, and more! $17.95 list, 8½x11, 160p, order no. 1092.

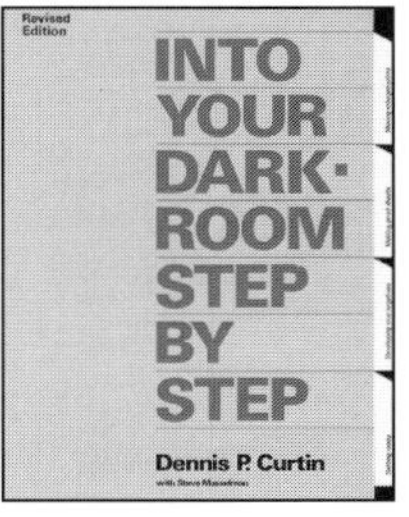

Into Your Darkroom Step-by-Step

Dennis P. Curtin

The ideal beginning darkroom guide. Easy to follow and fully illustrated each step of the way. Information on: equipment you'll need, set-up, making proof sheets and much more! $17.95 list, 8½x11, 90p, hundreds of photos, order no. 1093.

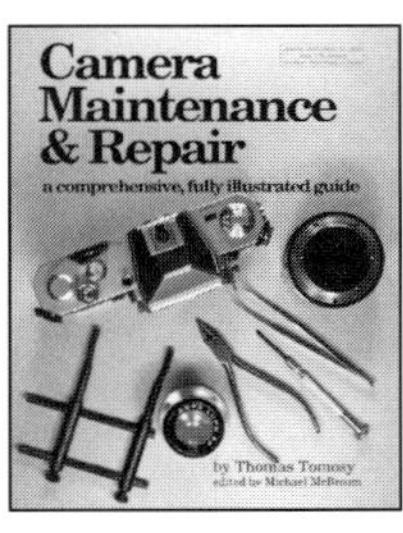

Camera Maintenance & Repair

Thomas Tomosy

A step-by-step, fully illustrated guide by a master camera repair technician. Sections include: testing camera functions, general maintenance, basic tools needed, basic repairs for accessories, camera electronics, plus "quick tips" for maintenance and more! $24.95 list, 8½x11, 176p, order no. 1158.

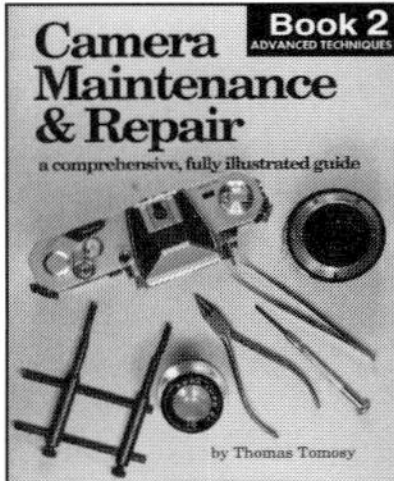

Camera Maintenance & Repair Book 2

Thomas Tomosy

Advanced troubleshooting and repair building on the basics covered in the first book. Includes; mechanical and electronic SLRs, zoom lenses, medium format, troubleshooting, repairing plastic and metal parts, and more. $29.95 list, 8½x11, 176p, 150+ photos, charts, tables, appendices, index, glossary, order no. 1558.

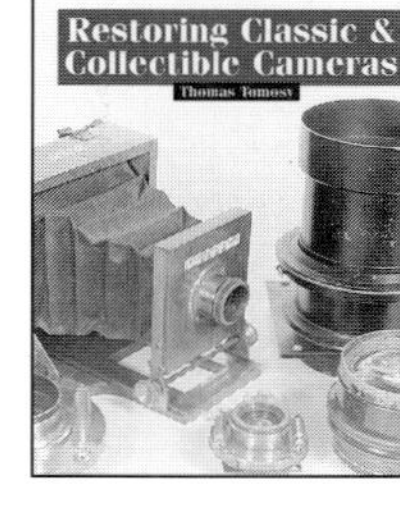

Restoring Classic & Collectible Cameras

Thomas Tomosy

A must for camera buffs and collectors! Clear, step-by-step instructions show how to restore a classic or vintage camera. Work on leather, brass and wood to restore your valuable collectibles. $34.95 list, 8½x11, 128p, b&w photos and illustrations, glossary, index, order no. 1613.

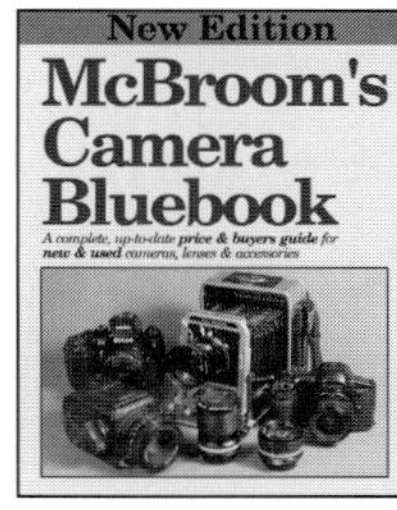

McBroom's Camera Bluebook

Mike McBroom

Comprehensive, fully illustrated, with pricing on: 35mm cameras, medium & large format cameras, exposure meters, strobes and accessories. Pricing info based on equipment condition. A must for any camera buyer, dealer, or collector! $34.95 list, 8½x11, 224p, 75+ photos, order no. 1263.

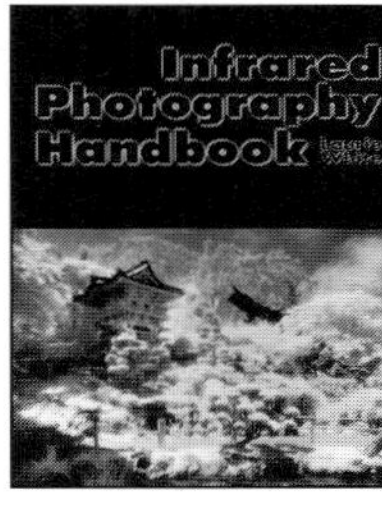

Infrared Photography Handbook

Laurie White

Covers b&w infrared photography: focus, lenses, film loading, film speed rating, heat sensitivity, batch testing, paper stocks, and filters. Photos illustrate IR film use in portrait, landscape, and architectural photography. $24.95 list, 8½x11, 104p, 50 b&w photos, charts & diagrams, order no. 1419.

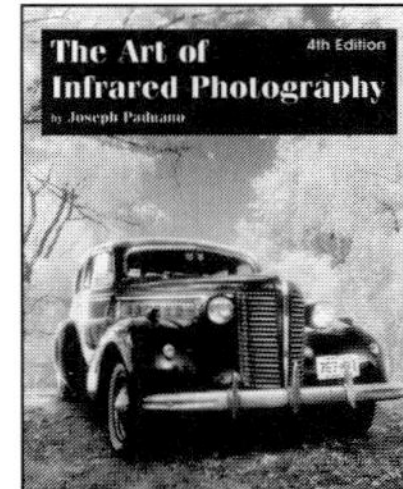

The Art of Infrared Photography / 4th Edition

Joe Paduano

A practical, comprehensive guide to infrared photography. Tells what to expect and how to control results. Includes: anticipating effects, color infrared, digital infrared, using filters, focusing, developing, printing, handcoloring, toning, and more! $29.95 list, 8½x11, 112p, order no. 1052.

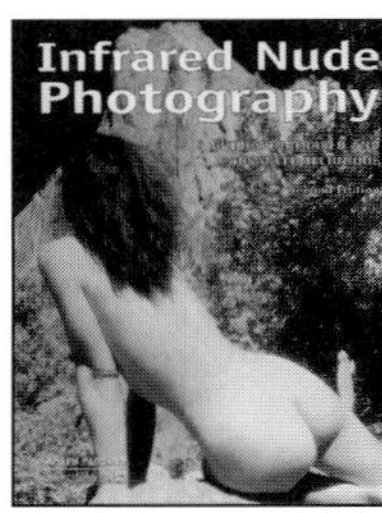

Infrared Nude Photography

Joseph Paduano

A stunning collection of images with informative how-to text. Over 50 infrared photos presented as a portfolio of classic nude work. Shot on location in natural settings, including the Grand Canyon, Bryce Canyon and the New Jersey Shore. $29.95 list, 8½x11, 96p, over 50 photos, order no. 1080.

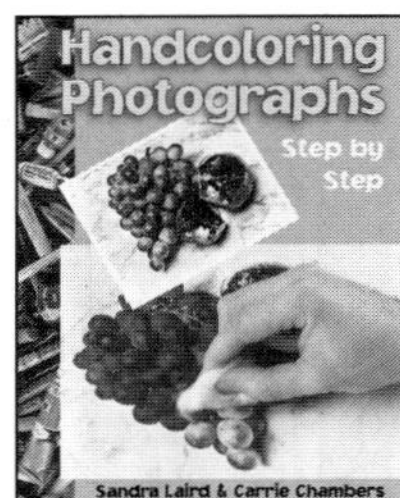

Handcoloring Photographs Step-by-Step

Sandra Laird & Carey Chambers

Learn to handcolor photographs step-by-step with the new standard handcoloring reference. Covers a variety of coloring media. Includes colorful photographic examples. $29.95 list, 8½x11, 112p, 100+ color and b&w photos, order no. 1543.

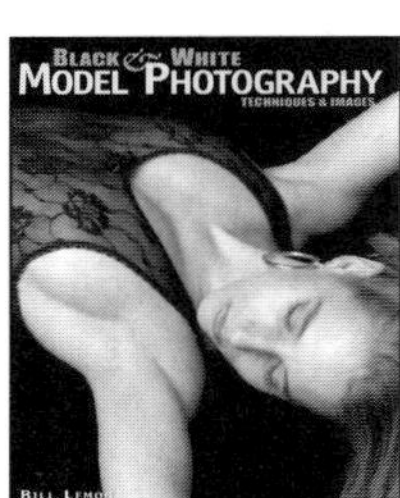

Black & White Model Photography

Bill Lemon

On location or in the studio, learn the techniques of a professional model photographer. Posing, lighting, equipment, model selection and composition are included. $29.95 list, 8½x11, 120p, 50+ b&w photos, order no. 1577.

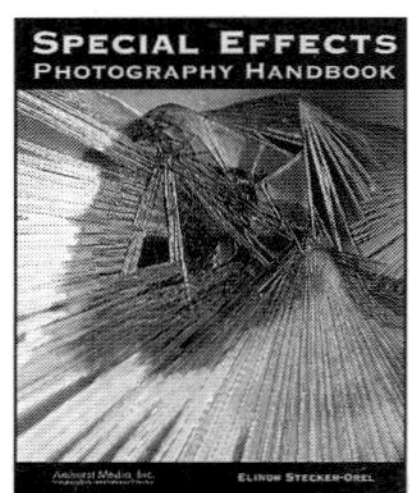

Special Effects Photography Handbook

Elinor Stecker Orel

Create magic on film with special effects! Little or no additional equipment required, use things you probably have around the house. Step-by-step instructions guide you through each effect. $29.95 list, 8½x11, 112p, 80+ color and b&w photos, index, glossary, order no. 1614.

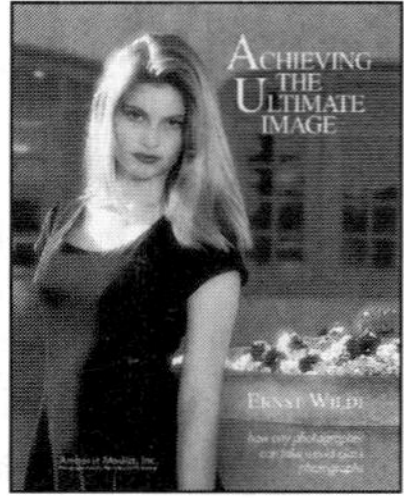

Achieving the Ultimate Image

Ernst Wildi

Ernst Wildi shows how any photographer can take world class photos and achieve the ultimate image. Features: exposure and metering, the Zone System, composition, evaluating an image, and much more! $29.95 list, 8½x11, 128p, 120 B&W and color photos, index, order no. 1628

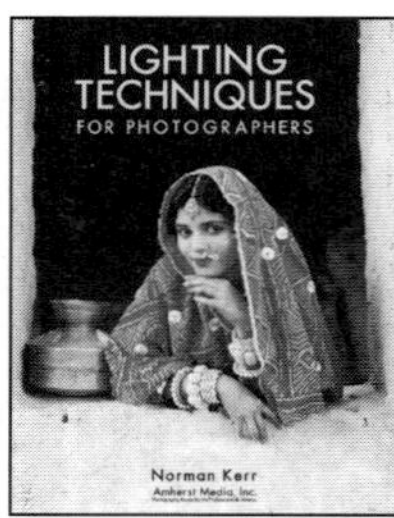

Lighting Techniques for Photographers

Norman Kerr

Learn to identify light qualities and control them to create dramatic images. Covers filters, choice of equipment, processing and composition for B&W and color images. $29.95 list, 8½x11, 120p, 100 B&W and color photos, index, order no. 1564.

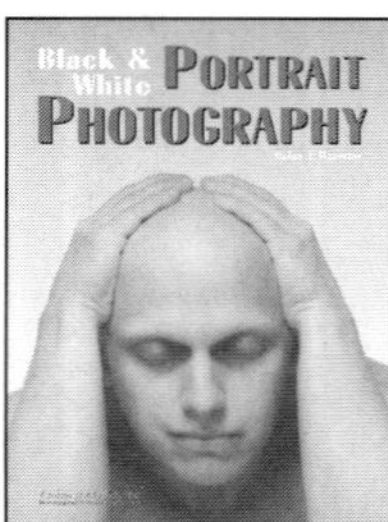

Black & White Portrait Photography

Helen Boursier

Make money with B&W portrait photography. Learn from top B&W shooters! Studio and location techniques, with tips on preparing your subjects, selecting settings and wardrobe, lab techniques, and more! $29.95 list, 8½x11, 128p, 130+ photos, index, order no. 1626.

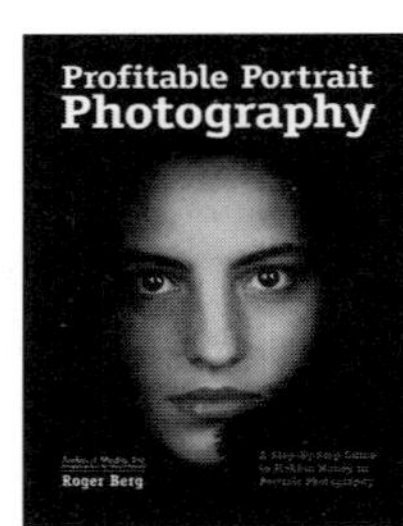

Profitable Portrait Photography

Roger Berg

Learn to profit in the portrait photography business! Improves studio methods, lighting techniques and posing, and tells how to get the best shot quickly. A step-by-step guide to making money. $29.95 list, 8½x11, 104p, 120+ B&W and color photos, index, order no. 1570.

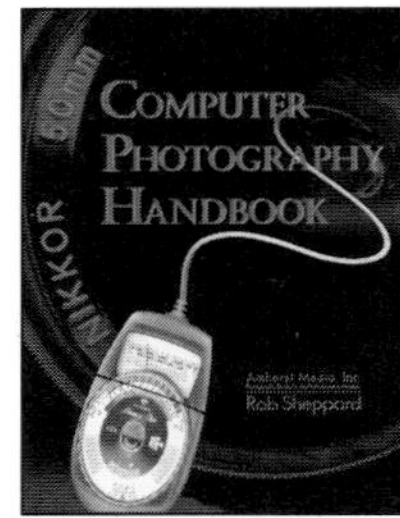

Computer Photography Handbook

Rob Sheppard

Learn to make the most of your photographs using computer technology! From creating images with digital cameras, to scanning prints and negatives, to manipulating images, you'll learn all the basics of digital imaging. $29.95 list, 8½x11, 128p, 150+ photos, index, order no. 1560.